THE BEDFORD SERIES IN HISTORY AND CULTURE

Candide

by Voltaire

Related Titles in
THE BEDFORD SERIES IN HISTORY AND CULTURE
Advisory Editors: Natalie Zemon Davis, Princeton University
Ernest R. May, Harvard University

The Secret by Francesco Petrarca (forthcoming)
Edited with an Introduction by Carol E. Quillen, *Rice University*

The Prince by Niccolò Machiavelli (forthcoming)
Translated, Edited, and with an Introduction by William J. Connell

Utopia by Sir Thomas More
Edited with an Introduction by David Harris Sacks, *Reed College*

The Discoverie of Guiana by Sir Walter Ralegh (forthcoming)
Edited with an Introduction by Benjamin Schmidt, *University of Washington*

*Jesuit Relations: Natives and Missionaries in
Seventeenth-Century North America* (forthcoming)
Allan Greer, *University of Toronto*

Louis XIV and Absolutism: A Brief History with Documents (forthcoming)
William Beik, *Emory University*

The Enlightenment: A Reader (forthcoming)
An Introduction with Texts by Margaret C. Jacob, *University of Pennsylvania*

*The Enlightenment Debate on Equality:
Wollstonecraft versus Rousseau* (forthcoming)
Edited with an Introduction by Olwen Hufton, *The European Institute*

THE BEDFORD SERIES IN HISTORY AND CULTURE

Candide

by Voltaire

Translated, Edited, and with an Introduction by

Daniel Gordon

University of Massachusetts at Amherst

BEDFORD/ST. MARTIN'S   Boston   New York

For Bedford/St. Martin's
History Editor: Katherine Kurzman
Developmental Editor: Charisse Kiino
Production Supervisor: William Kirrane
Marketing Manager: Charles Cavaliere
Project Management: Books By Design, Inc.
Text Design: Claire Seng-Niemoeller
Cover Design: Donna Dennison
Cover Photo: The Crowning of Voltaire's Bust in the Théâtre Français, Paris, March 30, 1778. Corbis-Bettmann
Composition: ComCom, an R. R. Donnelley & Sons Company
Printing and Binding: Haddon Craftsmen, an R. R. Donnelley & Sons Company

President: Charles H. Christensen
Editorial Director: Joan E. Feinberg
Editor in Chief: Nancy Perry
Director of Editing, Design, and Production: Marcia Cohen
Manager, Publishing Services: Emily Berleth

Library of Congress Catalog Card Number: 98-85192

4   3   2   1   0   9
f   e   d   c   b   a

For information, write: Bedford/St. Martin's, 75 Arlington Street, Boston, MA 02116
(617-426-7440)

ISBN: 0–312–14854–2   (paperback)
ISBN: 0–312–21816–8   (hardcover)

Photo Credits
Page 35, Corbis-Bettmann; page 36, top, Corbis-Bettmann; page 36, bottom, Bulloz; page 37, Bulloz; page 38, top, Corbis-Bettmann; page 38, bottom, Roger-Viollet; page 39, Roger-Viollet.

Foreword

The Bedford Series in History and Culture is designed so that readers can study the past as historians do.

The historian's first task is finding the evidence. Documents, letters, memoirs, interviews, pictures, movies, novels, or poems can provide facts and clues. Then the historian questions and compares the sources. There is more to do than in a courtroom, for hearsay evidence is welcome, and the historian is usually looking for answers beyond act and motive. Different views of an event may be as important as a single verdict. How a story is told may yield as much information as what it says.

Along the way the historian seeks help from other historians and perhaps from specialists in other disciplines. Finally, it is time to write, to decide on an interpretation and how to arrange the evidence for readers.

Each book in this series contains an important historical document or group of documents, each document a witness from the past and open to interpretation in different ways. The documents are combined with some element of historical narrative—an introduction or a biographical essay, for example—that provides students with an analysis of the primary source material and important background information about the world in which it was produced.

Each book in the series focuses on a specific topic within a specific historical period. Each provides a basis for lively thought and discussion about several aspects of the topic and the historian's role. Each is short enough (and inexpensive enough) to be a reasonable one-week assignment in a college course. Whether as classroom or personal reading, each book in the series provides firsthand experience of the challenge—and fun—of discovering, recreating, and interpreting the past.

Natalie Zemon Davis
Ernest R. May

Preface

When *Candide* appeared in print in 1759, it shocked political and religious authorities all across Europe. The condemnations, confiscations, and burnings were of no avail: the book became a best-seller of the Enlightenment precisely because it was so radical and irreverent. Yet twentieth-century readers are often perplexed to find that *Candide* also contains a dark side. Instead of optimism, one finds a meditation on suffering. Instead of the idea of progress, one finds a philosophy that emphasizes limits. The book simply does not illustrate the standard definitions of the French Enlightenment that appear in textbooks and general histories. For this very reason, *Candide* is essential reading for those who wish to gain a more nuanced understanding of Voltaire and eighteenth-century thought.

In the introduction, I stress Voltaire's importance, in both his age and ours, as a symbol of the Enlightenment. But I also emphasize the complexity behind the symbol. *Candide* is the work of a man with a talent for playfully sustaining morbid memories and contradictory hopes. To help readers understand what Anatole France called Voltaire's "serene and smiling desolation," I relate Voltaire's life in terms of his anguish as well as his triumphs. I also take an argumentative approach. Instead of summarizing the points of consensus among Voltaire scholars or outlining in a neutral tone the points of debate, I take positions and make interpretations. I do not expect complete agreement from every reader; I only try to provide an example of active engagement with the author and his work.

Overall, the introduction is historical in method but appreciative in content. Voltaire was a man of the eighteenth century, and students must learn to interpret *Candide* in the context of the Old Regime. The introduction and related documents in this volume will help them do so. But Voltaire is also one of the enduring spirits of European civilization. Teachers, who must encourage students to respect literature and to think inside of it, will also find that the introduction raises perennial philosophical questions. The two goals—historical analysis and intellectual appreciation—are distinct enough to create a tension. But each is so important that the dilemma must be welcomed and sustained.

The translation in this volume follows principles that I discuss in detail in the "Note on Voltaire's Vocabulary and the Present Translation." Above all, I have tried to keep the text provocative. If *Candide* does not shock readers today, I believe this is due less to the passage of time than to the prudishness of certain English versions. The book is replete with intimations of sexual deviation. This innuendo touches not only the antagonists—the figures who oppress Candide, Cunégonde, and their friends—but also the protagonists themselves. *Candide* is a story with no virgin heroes. The key to understanding Voltaire's style is to be alert to his limitless irony, his delight in exposing impurity *everywhere*.

I am grateful to Natalie Zemon Davis for encouraging this project and to the fine editors at Bedford/St. Martin's, especially Katherine E. Kurzman, Sponsoring Editor, and Charisse Kiino, Developmental Editor. Several scholars and professional translators reviewed the manuscript, and their suggestions helped to bring about a text that is much improved over the first draft. David A. Bell, Suzanne Desan, Nina Rattner Gelbart, Lynn Hunt, Edgar Leon Newman, Jeffrey S. Ravel, and Isser Woloch read the introduction. Robert D. Cottrell, Jeffrey Mehlman, Steven Rendall, and Carol Stopforth read the translation. I thank them all. Their participation, of course, does not imply that they accept all formulations. Any scandalous errors or indignities in this volume are due entirely to me—or to Voltaire.

Daniel Gordon

Contents

Foreword   v

Preface   vii

PART ONE

Introduction: The Paradoxes of Voltaire   1

The Duality of Voltaire   2

Voltaire and the Old Regime   5
Absolute Monarchy   6
Nobility   8
Religion   10

Candide   15
The Unhappy Voltaire   15
Voltaire against Leibniz   18
Ridicule, Sex, Irony   24

Note on Voltaire's Vocabulary and the Present Translation   31

ILLUSTRATIONS   35

PART TWO

Candide, or Optimism   41

PART THREE
Related Documents 121

Voltaire, *Letter to Catherine-Olympe du Noyer,*
November 28, 1713 121

Voltaire, *Letter to Frederick, Crown Prince of Prussia,*
October 15, 1737 122

Voltaire, *Letter to François-Thomas-Marie de Baculard d'Arnaud,*
October 14, 1749 126

Voltaire, *Letter to Jean-Robert Tronchin,* November 24, 1755 127

Omer Joly de Fleury, *Letter to Henry-Léonard-Jean-Baptiste Bertin,*
February 24, 1759 128

Voltaire, *Letter to Gabriel and Philibert Cramer,*
February 25, 1759 128

Elie Fréron, *Review of* Candide, 1759 129

APPENDICES

A Voltaire Chronology (1694–1791)   132
Questions for Consideration   134
Selected Bibliography   135

Index of Key Concepts   137

Candide

by Voltaire

PART ONE

Introduction: The Paradoxes of Voltaire

Eighteenth-century Europe is often called the Age of Voltaire. What is astonishing is that this expression was already common in Voltaire's lifetime.[1] He was the first writer to become the symbol of his age—to his age. As a young man, he was hailed by the French literary establishment as the most gifted poet in the nation. In his middle years, he turned against authority and became the first critic of religious extremism, the first defender of human rights, to appeal to a mass audience in several countries. As an elderly man, this impious crusader became the object of a cult with fanatical overtones of its own.

Voltaire died at the age of 83 and was combative to the end. He took part in nearly every major controversy of his time. While engaging the external world, he challenged himself too: he evolved as a human being and underwent profound changes in his philosophy. He was also remarkably prolific. The modern edition of his writings fills more than 135 volumes.[2] On account of his productivity and complexity, Voltaire eludes simple textbook classifications. The purpose of this introduction is to avoid easy definitions; to draw attention to Voltaire's unconventional acts and volatile ideas; and even to bring out the contradictions in his thought,

---

[1] André Magnan, "Siècle de Voltaire," in *Inventaire Voltaire,* ed. Jean Goulemot, André Magnan, Didier Masseau (Paris: Gallimard, 1995), 1252.

[2] *The Complete Works of Voltaire,* ed. Theodore Besterman (Geneva: Institut et Musée Voltaire, 1968–1977).

which, far from being an embarassment to him, are the true emblems of his brilliance.

An introduction, of course, is just a beginning. In the end readers must forge their own opinions of Voltaire. There is still much debate about *Candide,* not only about its value as a work of literature and philosophy but also about the very meaning of the text. Interpretation, however, is not an entirely subjective matter. To know about the life of an author, the society in which he or she lived, and the controversies of the time—all of these things help to place a book in proper perspective. And only by viewing a work in this historical manner can we begin to appreciate it fully, or to criticize it responsibly.

THE DUALITY OF VOLTAIRE

Voltaire was born in Paris in 1694. After studying at a boarding school run by Jesuit priests, he rebelled against his father's efforts to turn him into a lawyer and devoted himself to quenching his thirst for sensuality and literary fame. "He slipped like an eel into all the places where pleasure was prized," noted Gustave Lanson, one of Voltaire's great biographers.[3] In 1718 his first play, *Oedipus,* retold the ancient story of the Theban prince who killed his father and slept with his mother. Composed in poetic verse, the dialogue of this play alluded to outrageous acts in impeccably refined language. *Oedipus* was an immediate success: it set a record for consecutive performances of a tragic play that was unsurpassed in Paris in the eighteenth century.[4] But Voltaire's straight path to glory was blocked by his own impetuous character. While he longed for success, he also had a compulsion to shock the high and mighty. He had already been imprisoned in 1717 for a poem implying that the regent of France[5] committed incest with his daughter. In the early 1720s he composed poems attacking Christianity. He kept them secret, but a public explosion of his passion for creating scandal was inevitable.

It occurred in 1726. The chevalier de Rohan, a member of a powerful noble family, poked fun at Voltaire's name as they passed each other in the opera. Voltaire, who was not a noble, boldly replied that the chevalier was a disgrace to his family name, whereas his own name would soon be famous throughout Europe. The next day, the chevalier's servants bru-

---

[3]Gustave Lanson, *Voltaire* (Paris: Hachette, 1906), 16.

[4]Theodore Besterman, *Voltaire* (New York: Harcourt, Brace & World, 1969), 73–74.

[5]Louis XIV died in 1715. Because his successor, Louis XV, was only five years old, a regency, or temporary rulership, was entrusted to Louis XIV's nephew, Philippe d'Orléans.

tally beat Voltaire with a stick. When Voltaire sought justice from the police, he found that his accuser's noble status placed him beyond reach. When his patrons in high society also showed him no sympathy, Voltaire purchased weapons and began to plan his own revenge. At this point the authorities intervened, imprisoned him, and promised to release him only if he left the country. So began Voltaire's life as exile and social critic. He lived most of his eighty-four years in places far from Paris, places where he was safe from arrest, either in the French provinces or in foreign countries. He still produced literature, but he used it to draw attention to prejudice and to defend its victims: "I write in order to act."[6]

This is an important statement. Once he left Paris, Voltaire abandoned the writer's traditional ambition to forge timeless works that would be appreciated forever by posterity. This literary ideal prevented writers from describing in specific terms the conditions and controversies of their own times. Authors aspiring to immortality tried to tell stories that contained universal themes and avoided the passing incidents of the present. But for Voltaire, the only person worthy of being recalled in the future is the one who gives everything to the present. Genuinely touched by the suffering of others, he was willing to descend into journalism and to saturate even his most ambitious literary works with references to the social and political issues of his time. Voltaire called this commitment to the present *humanité* (humanity).[7]

To idealize Voltaire as a great humanitarian would be to oversimplify his life, for as we will see, his personality was many-sided. It is nonetheless true that Voltaire pioneered the role of the modern intellectual who mocks tradition, disdains organized religion, and seeks to redeem himself by serving as the conscience of his age—and the response he got from his age was enormous. In 1778, at the request of numerous supporters, the elderly Voltaire returned triumphantly to Paris after many years of exile. In the course of festivities in his honor, the directors of the leading playhouse, the *Comédie Française,* placed a bust of him inside the theater. In doing so they violated a tradition according to which only deceased authors could be immortalized with a statue in this hallowed building. With the unveiling of this icon, the present suddenly became posterity. Voltaire, already a symbol of his own age, had the pleasure of seeing himself resurrected in advance for the next. The ecstasy of his supporters is evident from a report in one of the newsletters of the period:

[6]Letter to Vernes, 15 April 1767; *Correspondence and Related Documents,* ed. Theodore Besterman (Geneva: Institut et Musée Voltaire, 1968–1977), 116:53.
[7]Voltaire, in fact, claimed to be one of the first persons to use the word *humanité*; see letter to Palissot, 4 June 1760; *Correspondence,* 105:350.

"The theater at this moment was perfectly transformed into a public place in which one had erected a monument to the glory of genius . . . . Envy and hatred, fanaticism and intolerance did not dare to cry out except in secret; and for perhaps the first time in France, one saw public opinion enjoy the splendor of its full authority."[8]

The story of the statue is an example of how Voltaire gave his admirers the exhilarating sentiment of living in an unprecedented era in history, an era in which one could set aside tradition and forge a new society on new foundations. Voltaire and other writers of his time affirmed that progress was unfolding and that theirs was a century of "reason" and "light." "The Age of Reason" and "the Enlightenment" are thus two terms we have inherited (along with "the Age of Voltaire") to describe the creative energy of the eighteenth century. In fact, we have inherited the spirit of the period as well as its self-descriptive terms; for we continue to live in a time that appreciates independence, criticism, and change. Who does not dream of achieving security and fame through one's own efforts, like Voltaire the self-made man of letters? Who does not desire to see the world become a happier place, like Voltaire the humanitarian reformer? And who does not believe that reason is an instrument of progress, like Voltaire the implacable critic of prejudice and superstition?

We are the heirs of Voltaire . . . yet it is not so simple. We are also strangers to him. He was, after all, a Frenchman of the Old Regime. His impact is incomprehensible without some knowledge of that remote time. To know him better, we will have to make a tour through France in the age of absolute monarchy. But there is more. The real Voltaire was not just the reflection of the Age of Reason. He was an enigmatic individual— calculating and passionate, imperious and vulnerable, self-righteous and self-critical. As a thinker he was more subtle than most of his contemporaries ever noticed. While striving to understand the Enlightenment that Voltaire symbolized, we must also seek to understand what he alone experienced and had to say.

To preserve a sense of Voltaire's complexity, it is useful to keep in mind this double nature of his identity. On the one hand, he was a celebrity: the leader of the Enlightenment and a symbol of the liberation of humankind through reason. In this role he coined the slogan *Écrasez l'infâme!* (Crush the vile thing!) "The vile thing" meant, above all, the bigotry of the Catholic Church, which Voltaire detested. But it also included anyone who promoted intolerance, torture, and murder. Many of

---

[8]*Correspondance littéraire, philosophique et critique . . . par le baron de Grimm et par Diderot,* 30 March 1778, 2nd ed. (Paris: F. Buison, 1812), 4:180.

Voltaire's writings are witty and courageous denunciations of the perpetrators of senseless violence.

On the other hand, Voltaire was a skeptic, overwhelmed by long periods of doubt and pessimism. He never entirely believed in the Enlightenment that he symbolized. *Candide* (first published in 1759) is a perfect expression of Voltaire's double identity. As a weapon of propaganda, it is filled with indignation against religious extremism and political injustice. Yet, as a spiritual meditation, it expresses Voltaire's rejection of the idea that evil can be eliminated from the world. Though the book contains much criticism, it is ultimately a confession in which Voltaire stresses the limits of human intelligence and the dangers of applying abstract ideals to everyday life.

Candide thus sustains a duality, or what might be called a deliberate bifurcation of thought. A closer look at Voltaire in relationship to the French society in which he lived reveals a similar splitting of consciousness. He was rarely for or against something entirely but was usually both for and against. He rebelled against the dominant institutions, but he simultaneously accepted the given structures of society. The greatest critic of his time, he had no utopian expectations. He died more than ten years before the Revolution of 1789; had he lived to see it, he probably would not have supported it. This paradoxical combination of struggle and conservatism, criticism and reconciliation, is the hallmark of Voltaire's posture as an intellectual living in the period of French history known as the Old Regime.

VOLTAIRE AND THE OLD REGIME

While the phrase "the Century of Voltaire" was used in Voltaire's century, the phrase "the Old Regime" was never used in the Old Regime. The term was first used during the French Revolution to designate the traditional society that the revolutionaries detested and wanted to annihilate. Though historians now refer to the Old Regime in a more neutral way, simply to refer to the two hundred years or so before 1789, the term still denotes a specific form of society based on the principle of hierarchy. The Old Regime was hierarchical in the political sphere because sovereignty was invested in an absolute monarch. It was hierarchical in the social sphere because prestige and economic advantages inhered in the nobility. And it was hierarchical in the religious sphere because Catholicism was the only religion officially permitted in France. This was the world that Voltaire tried to change, but it was also the world that he took for granted.

Absolute Monarchy

The French monarchy dated back to the early Middle Ages, but by the time Voltaire was born, this old institution had taken on a new form, that of *absolute* monarchy. Officially, all power rested in the king. In contrast to England's constitutional monarchy, the French system had no parliamentary elections and no political parties which openly competed for power. Theorists of French absolutism (and Voltaire was sometimes one of them) emphasized that any opposition to the Crown was likely to degenerate into massive and unstoppable violence. This argument was grounded in the experiences of the sixteenth and early seventeenth centuries.

Following the Protestant Reformation of the early sixteenth century, France had been ravaged for decades by religious war. In the midst of this continuous bloodshed, political philosophers such as Jean Bodin, author of *The Six Books of the Commonwealth* (1576), claimed that the only way to bring about peace among religious enemies was for everyone to defer to the all-powerful authority of the state. The community, according to Bodin, could achieve stability only by accepting the government's right "to impose laws generally on all subjects regardless of their consent."[9] Throughout the seventeenth and eighteenth centuries, spokesmen for the Crown repeated this principle. They developed the logic of absolutism even further by stressing the antisocial dimensions of human nature. Nicolas Delamare, the author of *A Treatise on Police* (1705), affirmed that ordinary people always acted on the basis of "self-love." He concluded that good laws were never enough to bind the populace. The essential thing was to have a "powerful authority to oversee their enforcement at all times."[10]

It followed from these principles that the king was the only "public" person. In other words, the capacity for making decisions about the common good belonged to him alone. Defenders of absolutism stressed that private citizens were capable of representing only their own selfish interests and had no right to gather in the marketplace or in clubs to discuss current events among themselves. Not just political gatherings but voluntary assemblies of any kind were inherently threatening to the Crown, even if they were peaceful. In fact, they were especially threatening if they were peaceful, because sociability implied that the king was superfluous, that human solidarity was possible without his command—and this is exactly what absolutist theorists claimed was impossible.

---

[9]Jean Bodin, *The Six Books of the Commonwealth* [first published in 1576], ed. M. J. Tooley (New York, 1955), 32.
[10]Nicolas Delamare, *Traité de la police,* 2nd ed. (Amsterdam, 1729), 1:246.

During the rulership of Louis XIV (1661–1715), the principles of absolute monarchy found their greatest expression in practice. Louis expanded the frontiers of France and carried the centralized system of his predecessors to its logical conclusion. He regarded the state as a cultural force as well as a political one. To destroy provincial differences and impose a uniform civilization was his goal. The center of this civilization was the court of Versailles, a town near Paris where Louis established the government in 1682. The refined etiquette at Versailles—its formal rules for table manners, conversation, and entertainment—shaped the tone of all other courts in Europe.

Many scenes in *Candide* take place in the New World, so it is worth noting that Louis's policies brought about the strong French presence there. His chief advisor, Colbert, ran the departments of commerce, colonies, and the navy. In 1664 Colbert founded the Company of the West, which monopolized trade with the West Indies, America, and Africa. A four-zone system developed in which slaves taken in West Africa were forced to labor on sugar and tobacco plantations in the West Indies. America provided foodstuffs for the slaves, and all three areas supplied Europe with raw materials for manufacturing.

Readers of *Candide* will have no trouble seeing that Voltaire regarded slavery as an outrage. That is enough to prove that he never accepted Louis XIV's legacy without question. Although he admired the power and prestige of the government that the Sun King established, he reserved the right to deplore any particular law or policy. As a critic whose works kindled political debate, Voltaire violated the principle that the king is the only public person. Yet, the fact remains: like most Enlightenment thinkers, Voltaire believed that monarchy was the only sensible form of government. He despised ignorance wherever he saw it, especially in the masses, and never imagined that the people could govern themselves in a large nation. In short, he was no democrat. He even wrote a laudatory history of the reign of Louis XIV, drawing special attention to the ways in which Louis stimulated literature and culture. While he supported freedom of religion, freedom of the press, the abolition of torture, and limits on the slave trade, Voltaire believed that only the king had enough power to implement such reforms effectively. Only a very strong state, he thought, could repress any opposition that might arise against these enlightened policies.

Voltaire's political outlook is a world away from that of Jean-Jacques Rousseau, the author of *The Social Contract* (1762). Rousseau, a democrat, dreamed of transferring absolute authority from the king to the people. Voltaire wished only to temper authority with humane principles. Liberal absolutism (or enlightened absolutism) is the best label for Voltaire's political philosophy.

Nobility

Imagine a young man of the middle class who hates his prosperous and disapproving father so much that he changes his last name. In selecting the new name he decides to give himself a noble image. That is exactly what Voltaire did at the age of twenty-three: he changed his name from François-Marie Arouet to François-Marie de Voltaire. The "de," known as the particle, is the sign of noble lineage in France. Eventually, Voltaire acquired a large estate with servants and lived the life of a privileged man. He was never truly a nobleman, but there was growing disagreement in the Old Regime about how to define membership in the nobility. Taking double advantage of the disintegration of feudal society, Voltaire became a part of the elite and then ripped it apart with criticism.

According to feudal tradition, the nobility was a hereditary order whose function was to defend the kingdom in wartime. The tax exemptions that elevated the nobles above the rest of the population were its compensation for protecting the realm. Other privileges included the right to be saluted by commoners, the right to seek satisfaction for an insult by fighting a duel, and the right to go hunting in order to exercise their warrior skills in peacetime.

Writers in the sixteenth and seventeenth centuries often asserted that this "nobility of the sword" was a race possessing special virtues:

> Nobility is a quality which makes generous whoever possesses it and which inwardly disposes the soul toward the love of worthy things. The virtue of a man's ancestors confers this excellent imprint of nobility. There is in the seed I know not what power or principle which transmits and continues the inclinations of fathers among their descendants.[11]

Yet in this same period the nobility underwent great change. First, in the sixteenth century, judges in the royal courts called *parlements* received permission from the King to acquire noble titles. In the seventeenth century, these judges were allowed to pass their titles on to their children. The "nobility of the robe," as it is called, thus became hereditary.

But the complications did not stop there. Louis XIV did more than any other monarch to undermine the independence of both the old nobility of the sword and the new nobility of the robe. To encourage loyalty to the state, he ennobled many commoners who acted as functionaries in his government. And in moments of financial difficulty, he simply sold

---

[11]Gilles André de la Roque, *Traité de la noblesse,* Preface to the 1678 edition (Paris: Mémoire et Documents, 1994), 23.

titles of nobility to financiers. Louis was not the inventor of these venal practices, but he expanded the system enormously. The sale of offices on a large scale was an insult to the *gentilhommes* — the great nobles who traced their lineage back many generations. Louis justified it by saying that people who gave money to the state deserved as much respect as people who fought to defend it.[12] He considered nobility a creation of the government and a reward for any service that the king deemed useful.

The subordination of the noble class to the interests of the Crown was one of the great historical trends of the seventeenth and eighteenth centuries. Louis XIV accelerated it more than any other ruler, but it continued throughout the Old Regime. Since it raised fundamental questions about the relationship between state and social status, it was a topic of continuous debate in the Enlightenment. Montesquieu, a member of the robe nobility and author of *The Persian Letters* (1721) and *The Spirit of the Laws* (1748), believed that France was becoming a despotic country with no checks on royal power. He supported the sale of titles of nobility because it expanded the noble class and infused it with new wealth. But Montesquieu bemoaned the fact that many nobles were abandoning their localities and forgetting their responsibility to protect the liberties of ordinary people. He was disgusted by the many nobles who were taking up residence in the court of Versailles and pandering to the king. Montesquieu regretted the decline of a proud and feisty nobility, which he saw as the protector of the people and the best check on royal despotism.

Voltaire did not share Montesquieu's idealized image of a distinguished and independent nobility. He regarded the provincial nobility as uncouth, ignorant, and absurdly proud of its lineage — as the beginning of *Candide* caustically shows. He was seized by an intense hatred of the whole concept of hereditary nobility, calling it "a monstrous insult to the human race because it assumes that some men are created with purer blood than the rest." He also considered the sale of titles to be absurd because it allowed mediocrities to enter the nobility: "In France, anyone can become a marquis who wants to be."[13] Overall, Voltaire detested the nobility. When he changed his name to de Voltaire, it was not an attempt to convince others that he came from a noble family: everyone knew very well that he did not. It was instead a gesture of defiance and flamboyant

[12]Roland Mousnier, *The Institutions of France under the Absolute Monarchy* (Chicago: University of Chicago Press, 1979), 1:127.

[13]A good discussion of Voltaire's attitude toward nobility is Jean Goulemot's "Noblesse," in *Inventaire Voltaire*, 970–71. The two quotations, the first from Voltaire's posthumously published notebooks and the second from his *Letters from England* (1733), are cited in this article.

self-esteem, as if he were saying, "I am as noble as anyone else because I am a genius and because I am going to be the greatest writer in Europe."

Although Voltaire hated the nobility, something also drew him toward it: he admired greatness and wished to be counted among the great. He could never distance himself entirely from the elite. He was fascinated, for example, by the heroism and intellectual refinement that the grandest nobles exhibited. In 1749 he published a funeral oration commemorating the courageous lords who died on the battlefield during the War of the Austrian Succession (1740–48).[14] It was also in 1749 that Voltaire's beloved mistress, Émilie du Châtelet, died in childbirth. Brilliant in her own right, she introduced Voltaire to the study of metaphysics and natural science. She belonged to the nobility. She was also married. Her aristocratic husband tolerated Voltaire's presence amicably. She even had a third lover, the writer Saint-Lambert, who was responsible for her fatal pregnancy! In certain circles of the French nobility there was an acceptance of sexual freedom and a deep respect for men of letters. Voltaire, who was a free spirit and believed in the nobility of the pen, was most at home among the upper crust.

Religion

While Voltaire had a love-hate relationship with the nobility, his attitude toward the Catholic Church was one of uninterrupted hostility. He once informed the English poet Alexander Pope that his Jesuit teachers had sexually used him when he was a schoolboy and that he would never get over it.[15] Several of his writings were burned by the Church on account of his audacious criticism of the whole Catholic hierarchy, including even the popes. The animosity between Voltaire and the clergy was so intense that after Voltaire died, some conservatives began to spread the vicious rumour that endured well into the nineteenth century: that Voltaire on his deathbed refused to make confession and that he languished in a state of animality, consuming his own excrement.[16]

Voltaire's hatred of the Jesuits may have stemmed from his years in a Jesuit school, but his systematic anticlericalism was above all a reaction against the enormous power wielded by the Catholic Church. Under the Old Regime there was no separation of church and state, and no concept of religious equality. The monarchy was sacred, which meant that the

---

[14]*Éloge funèbre des officiers qui sont morts dans la guerre de 1741.*

[15]A.-M. Rousseau, *L'Angleterre et Voltaire,* published in *Studies in Voltaire and the Eighteenth Century,* vol. 145 (1976), 113.

[16]André Magnan, "Excrément," in *Inventaire Voltaire,* 517.

king ruled by "divine right" and was obligated to promote Catholicism among his subjects. King Henri IV had granted some toleration to Protestants in the Edict of Nantes (1598). But Louis XIV, at the height of his power in the 1680s, confidently set out to overturn the edict, believing that he could eliminate Protestantism without risking a dangerous civil war. He succeeded. In 1682 he issued edicts closing Protestant churches and schools. Troops appeared in town after town, officially requesting Protestants to convert voluntarily to Catholicism, but actually threatening them with death or separation from their families. Finally, in 1685 came the Revocation of the Edict of Nantes. All Protestant ministers were expelled and all Protestant churches ordered to be demolished. Hundreds of thousands of the faithful emigrated along with their pastors. Many of the converts who stayed behind practiced their old religion in secret; but as a public faith, Protestantism was crushed.[17]

If we turn from the treatment of non-Catholics to the internal structure of the French Catholic Church, it is striking how many privileges and powers it possessed, yet how divided it was at the same time. Like the nobility, the clergy was exempt from most forms of taxation. In fact, it levied its own tax, the tithe, which was essentially a portion of the gross agricultural product — grain, wine, sheep, and so forth — that any peasant produced. The Church also had its own sphere of disciplinary authority. Though the king had the power to appoint bishops, the bishops claimed the right to decide all questions relating to faith and morals and to punish "heresy," that is, stubborn attachment to an idea or action condemned by the Church. Punishment could be a fine, public penance, confiscation of property, or death. Heretics were also denied Christian burial and thrown in the garbage dump. In *Candide* the dump is mentioned several times. This persistent image reveals Voltaire's fear that he would end up being buried in disgrace. (The fear was well grounded. When Voltaire died on May 30, 1778, the Archbishop of Paris tried to prevent a Christian burial. But friends of Voltaire smuggled the corpse out of Paris. A priest named Mignot, who was Voltaire's great-nephew, arranged for the body to be buried with proper ceremony in the abbey of Scellières, in Champagne.)

In contrast to the nobility, the clergy was not a hereditary class; the

---

[17]Beginning in the 1760s, the anti-Protestant edicts were enforced less severely. This was partly due to the influence of Enlightenment thinkers like Voltaire who advocated religious liberty. In 1787 Louis XVI formally recognized the right of Protestants to live, work, contract marriages, and worship in private on French soil. But they were still excluded from holding administrative and judicial appointments. Only with the Revolution did religious minorities gain civic equality.

church had to recruit young priests from outside. It was an attractive profession because it provided authority and income. Some members of the clergy joined for profit and had only elementary notions of Catholic theology. They drank heavily, frequented prostitutes, engaged in brawls, and routinely skipped Mass. The inhabitants of certain parishes were so accustomed to the promiscuity of their priests that they had no idea that the clergy was supposed to be celibate.[18] Voltaire loved to satirize the hypocrisy of this impious clergy, which exercised religious authority but not religion.

Many, probably most, clergymen, however, were filled with a sense of duty. The Jesuits often stood out in this respect. The Jesuits were an order of monks but they minimized the solitary duties of the cloister and participated actively in the social and political life of the nation. They saw themselves as soldiers using all possible means to fight for the Catholic Church. One of these means was education. Supremely well-educated themselves, the Jesuits established schools across France that provided the best instruction to boys from the upper classes. The oldest and most famous was the *Collège de Clermont* in Paris, which Voltaire attended from age ten to sixteen. The rigorous Jesuit curriculum emphasized languages and literature—the arts of communication. Ironically, the Jesuits were the first to kindle Voltaire's passion for the writer's craft. They provided him with the literary and philosophical tools that he would eventually sharpen on his own and use to lacerate his teachers.

Thanks to their ambition and superior education, the Jesuits acquired considerable influence in France. Many bishops and royal confessors belonged to their order. But the Jesuits were vulnerable on one point: they swore absolute allegiance to the pope, and after him, to the father general of all the Jesuits in Europe. They were thus open to the charge of disloyalty to the French monarchy, an accusation raised often by their opponents, the Jansenists.

In *Candide* Voltaire alludes several times to the Jansenists and their rivalry with the Jesuits. The Jansenists were Catholics but their religious beliefs resembled Calvinist Protestantism in important ways. They considered grace to be a pure gift of God, not a reward for good deeds. And they disapproved of the wordly lifestyle of courtiers and rich Jesuit prelates. The struggle between Jansenists and Jesuits raged from the early eighteenth century onward. Obeying a papal order against Jansenism, the Bull Unigenitus (1713), the Jesuits and other Catholic priests aggressively persecuted the Jansenists. In the 1740s and 1750s,

---

[18]Mousnier, 1:339.

the Church required dying persons to sign certificates called "bills of confession" stating that they were not Jansenists. Those who refused could be denied the last rites and proper burial. Voltaire ridicules these bills of confession in Chapter 22 of *Candide*.

Although the Jesuits were formally bound to support the Pope over the king, Louis XV trusted them and preferred them to the Jansenists. But Jansenism was popular among the judicial elite of France—the members of the parlements. A surge of judicial resistance beginning in the 1750s, along with growing hatred of the Jesuits among the public, pressured Louis XV to suppress the Jesuit order. In 1764 he issued an edict expelling the Jesuits from France. It was a dramatic setback for Europe's most militant religious order. And it was a setback for French absolutism too. While it revealed the supreme authority of the king—his power to expel whomever he wished—it also revealed the king's inability to control public opinion on matters of religion.

Voltaire's writings certainly played a role in discrediting the Jesuits. He understood that humor was the best way to destroy a group's prestige. Readers were delighted by the scene in *Candide* in which cannibals chant: "It's a Jesuit, it's a Jesuit . . . here's a good meal; let's eat Jesuit, let's eat Jesuit!"[19] Yet, there is more to Voltaire's religious thought than his rabid anticlericalism. While conducting a campaign of satire against Jesuits and religious fanatics of all kinds, Voltaire waged a second war: a war against atheism.

Voltaire firmly believed in God. Like many thinkers of the Enlightenment, he was a "deist." This means that he accepted the existence of a divine being who created the world, but did not accept the specifically Christian notion of the Trinity. He venerated Jesus but only as a man, a moral example, a teacher—not as the son of God. It was precisely because he admired Jesus that he abhorred the Catholic Church. (He was fond of saying that Jesus never had anyone burned for his religious views.) The essence of religion, as he saw it, was a belief in God and a conviction that God wants humans to be generous to each other. He considered all religions true to the degree that they promoted tolerance and fellowship, and false to the extent that they created hatred and division. "We need a God who speaks to the human race," he wrote.[20]

Around mid-century, Voltaire's religion began to look outdated to some of the younger and more radical philosophers of the Enlightenment,

---

[19]According to the Duc de La Vallière, "Let's eat Jesuit" instantly became a popular slogan in Paris. See his letter to Voltaire, Jan./Feb., 1759; *Correspondence,* 103:365.

[20]Voltaire to Elie Bertrand, 18 Feb., 1756; *Correspondence,* 101:73.

such as Julien Offroy de La Mettrie, the author of *Man A Machine*. La Mettrie was a doctor who insisted that the world, including human beings, is composed of physical matter and nothing else. He refused to accept the notion of a separate world of spirit. He even claimed that virtue did not exist because everything is physical and can thus be explained through mechanical causes. Voltaire found these ideas intolerable but difficult to refute. Sometimes he answered the materialists by arguing that atheism would destroy society if it became widespread. "If God did not exist it would be necessary to invent him" is his most famous pronouncement on religion.[21] In other words, society could not endure without religious belief, which binds people into a moral community.

This argument did not convince Voltaire's atheistic opponents—because it is not a convincing argument. The fact that society would crumble without belief in God does not prove that God exists. It only suggests that religious mythology has a beneficial social function. But Voltaire never defined religion as a false myth that happens to have useful consequences. His sentiment that God existed was genuine. He believed in what he invented. There is no escaping the conclusion that Voltaire, the symbol of the Age of Reason, was a man of passionate faith.

Considered as a whole, Voltaire's relationship to the Old Regime was many-sided and filled with paradoxes. One might say that he was a radical who tended to interpret his own ideas in the most conservative spirit possible. He criticized kings when they promoted injustice, but he defended kingship. He scorned the nobility, while cultivating connections with it. He attacked the Church, and tried to save the moral essence of Christianity. On many points he had to defend himself not only against apologists for the status quo but also against other thinkers of the Enlightenment, such as Rousseau, Montesquieu, and La Mettrie. Though they often paid homage to Voltaire as the symbol of independent reason, the philosophers of the Enlightenment disagreed among themselves, precisely because each wished to reason independently. The unity of reason that Voltaire symbolized never became a reality.

Yet that does not mean that Voltaire was a failure. The failure, if there was one, belonged to his admirers who were blind to the forces dividing the Enlightenment. They placed Voltaire on a pedestal as a symbol of their common longing for truth and progress. They avoided dwelling on their disagreements, on everything that threatened to blow their dream

---

[21]Voltaire composed this line in 1769. For fuller discussion, see André Magnan, "Si Dieu n'existait pas . . . ," in *Inventaire Voltaire*, 1246–47.

of a perfect new age into pieces. Voltaire himself was more lucid than that. As *Candide* shows, he had no illusions about himself as a savior of the human race.

CANDIDE

Candide is about the pursuit of happiness. Enlightenment philosophers often affirmed that human beings have a right to seek happiness in their own way. Voltaire believed this too. But in *Candide,* he is less concerned about defending the right to pursue happiness than he is about describing what really occurs—the result—when individuals embark on a quest for perfect bliss. The result, he suggests, is disaster.

The main character is a "youth" named Candide. His exact age is not given, but he is clearly in his late teens. In French, *candide* means naive and simple and thus suggests ignorance; but it also means candid and honest and thus suggests integrity. In the beginning of the story it is Candide's naiveté that stands out. He is utterly untutored in the ways of the world and all the suffering it contains. By the end, however, his candor has allowed him to receive an education. Thanks to his openness to new lessons, he is able to reconcile himself to the pain that he finds in the world, and in his own soul.

The Unhappy Voltaire

Every reader of *Candide* who has heard of Voltaire only as a leading thinker of the Enlightenment is astonished by the dark aspects of the tale. The inevitability of suffering, however, is one of the great themes of Voltaire's work. "The earth is a vast theater where the same tragedy is playing with different titles," he wrote in one of his historical works.[22] And in his notebooks: "Man is the only animal who knows that he will die. Sad knowledge, but unavoidable because he has ideas. There are thus sorrows necessarily attached to the condition of man."[23]

Voltaire could be hilariously gay and witty, but as these remarks show, he had a tendency to brood. Beginning in his late twenties, he became nervous about his health and certain that he would not live long. Voltaire was a tall, extremely thin man. His constitution was strong—he lived into

[22]Voltaire, *Essai sur les moeurs,* in *Oeuvres complètes* (Paris: Garnier Frères, 1877), 12:430.

[23]*Voltaire's Notebooks,* ed. Theodore Besterman (Geneva: Institut et Musée Voltaire, 1952), 2:352.

his eighties—but he always imagined himself to be on the verge of death. He consumed vast quantities of drugs and medicines and frequently began his letters by expressing astonishment that he was still alive: "I interrupt my agony to inform you . . . " "I am rising a little from my grave to tell you . . . " "I forgot to have myself buried . . . "

Besides this anxiety over his physical state, Voltaire was no stranger to emotional difficulties. All the fame in the world could not erase his recurrent bouts of gloom. In 1971, the influential literary critic Roland Barthes failed to take this into account when he mistakenly described Voltaire as "the last happy writer."[24] According to Barthes, Voltaire lived comfortably and had the luxury of believing that he was always right in his battles against injustice. Barthes claimed that Voltaire took for granted the existence of absolute "Good" and "Evil" and never worried about the validity of his own moral judgments. In the nineteenth century, Barthes argued, philosophers discovered the relative nature of all systems of thought, and from that time onward, all writers suffered from uncertainty—including uncertainty about the value of their own writing. Describing the Enlightenment as "outdated," Barthes consigned Voltaire to the trash heap of thinkers who failed to anticipate the problems of living in the modern age.

Barthes has influenced French studies in both France and America, but never has one brilliant writer so thoroughly misunderstood another. Voltaire was no stranger to unhappiness. His mother died when he was ten. At seventeen, when he was working as a secretary in the French embassy in Holland, he fell passionately in love with a Protestant girl named Pimpette. He tried to elope with her but was forced to return to France when Pimpette's mother complained to the embassy and when his own father threatened to deport him to America. Then there was the death in 1749 of Madame du Châtelet. She was his lover, friend, and intellectual partner all at once. Voltaire respected her as an equal and described her to his friends as "a great man."[25] When she died he declared, "I have not lost a mistress, I have lost half of myself."[26] Weeks later, his servants observed him waking up at night and calling for her from room to room.[27]

Being a humanitarian was not all joy either. In a sharp reply to Barthes,

---

[24]Roland Barthes, "The Last Happy Writer," in *Critical Essays* (Evanston, Ill.: Northwestern University Press, 1972; first published in French in 1971), 83–90.

[25]Letter to Fawkener, 2 March 1740; *Voltaire's Correspondence*, 91:118; and to d'Arnaud, 14 Oct. 1749, 95:179 (translated in this volume).

[26]Letter to d'Argental, 23 Sept. 1749, 95:167.

[27]Mason, *Voltaire*, 45.

Patrick Henry, an authority on Voltaire, noted that Voltaire's commitment to improving society was a painful struggle. Since he wished to improve the world, he was bound to be distressed when the world refused to improve.[28] And in fact Voltaire did lose many of his fights. An example is his unsuccessful effort to save the life of the British Admiral John Byng, who was condemned to death in 1757 for backing away from a naval battle. Voltaire's bitterness is clear in Chapter 23 of *Candide* when he describes the brutal execution. This is only one of many injustices portrayed in the tale that actually occurred and that touched Voltaire deeply.

Jean Starobinski, one of the great interpreters of eighteenth-century thought, has suggested that *Candide* presents the first global vision of suffering.[29] The tale does in fact give a panoramic view of disasters and atrocities on different continents. Mutilations, castrations, disembowelments, amputations, and rapes are everywhere. Every form of debasement of human life, from slavery to war to unbearable loneliness, is represented. *Candide* is a catalogue of suffering, comparable to Dante's *Inferno* in its completeness, except that the suffering takes place in this life, and Voltaire never suggests that things could be better in a world to come.

Voltaire did not just write about suffering; he suffered along with the victims. His extreme, visceral sympathy could even make him physically ill. Every year, on August 24, he became sick and could not rise from his bed. This was the anniversary of the St. Bartholomew's Day Massacre of 1572, when French Catholics murdered thousands of French Protestants in a fury of hatred.[30] In *Candide,* Voltaire's evocation of suffering is so intense that it is impossible to imagine him writing it in the spirit of self-satisfaction that Barthes and other anti-Enlightenment critics attribute to him. In Chapter 19, his empathy stretches across the color line as he reveals the pathetic image of an African slave whose limbs have been hacked off as punishment for trying to escape. In Chapter 24, he crosses the gender barrier in a poignant section about the degraded and hopeless life of a prostitute:

> Oh! Sir, if only you could imagine what it's like . . . to be exposed to every kind of insult and outrage; to be frequently reduced to borrowing a skirt so that some disgusting man can have the pleasure of lifting it; to be robbed by one man of what you've earned from another;

[28]Patrick Henry, "Contre Barthes," *Studies on Voltaire and the Eighteenth Century* (1987), vol. 249, 19–36.

[29]Jean Starobinski, "Voltaire's Double-Barreled Musket," in *Blessings in Disguise: The Morality of Evil* (Cambridge: Harvard University Press, 1993), 85.

[30]René Pomeau, *Voltaire* (Paris: Seuil, 1955), 39.

to be blackmailed by officers of the law; and to have no future in view except an atrocious old age, a hospital, and the public dump . . .

Voltaire's sympathy is unmistakable here, but so is his sense of futility and sadness.

Nevertheless, a portion of what Barthes said about Voltaire has to be considered more carefully. When Barthes affirmed that Voltaire was "happy," he meant two things. First, he meant that Voltaire's life was free of anguish, and we have seen that this view is simply uninformed. Second, Barthes meant that Voltaire was lucky because he lived in an age that naively took for granted that the universe had a clear moral structure. This view is also mistaken, but it is a far more complex issue—one that takes us deeply into Voltaire's philosophy.

The complexity of Voltaire's philosophy is often omitted from essays on *Candide,* especially those designed for students and nonspecialists. *Candide,* after all, is a story, not a dense philosophical treatise, so it seems that no technical background is necessary. Voltaire, however, wrote stories because he reached a point where it was clear to him that stories were the best way to approach philosophical questions that others had dealt with only in abstract treatises. The questions were: Why is there suffering in the world? And, what attitude should we take toward the imperfections of the universe? Voltaire himself worked on a long *Treatise on Metaphysics* in the 1730s, but he shifted to storytelling afterward. To understand his move from theory to narrative, from philosophy to literature, we must look into his struggle with one of the great thinkers of modern times.

Voltaire against Leibniz

Gottfried Wilhelm Leibniz (1646–1716) was the most universal genius of the era before Voltaire's ascendancy. Born in the German town of Leipzig, he was largely self-taught. He learned Latin on his own as a child and consumed books in law, philosophy, mathematics, and theology. At the age of twenty he wrote *De Arte Combinatoria* (On the Art of Combination) in which he maintained that all reasoning is reducible to an ordered combination of simple elements. He later constructed a calculating machine and perfected the binary system of numeration (i.e., using two as base). For this work he is seen as one of the forerunners of modern computer science. But that is only a small part of his intellectual achievement. As a mathematician, Leibniz laid the foundations of integral and differential calculus. As an engineer, he developed a water pump run by windmills; he worked on submarines, clocks, and many other devices. He is regarded as one of the creators of geology on account of his theory that the earth was at first molten.

Leibniz, however, was not just a scientist. He was a devout Protestant with a passion for understanding the world as God's creation. This passion took him into metaphysics (literally "beyond physics," the study of reality as a whole and the principles behind the existence of things). It was Leibniz's great dream to explain why all things are the way they are and, in so doing, to reconcile faith and science. He began with the assumption that God himself is a rational creature. Hence, to imitate God and to comprehend his creation, humans too must exercise their faculty of reason. Leibniz expressed this beautifully by saying that to be pious one must love God, but one cannot love God without knowing him. Religion and intellect are not mutually exclusive. One must enter into the mind of God and appreciate the glorious consistency of the world he created.[31]

According to Leibniz, if God is rational, then everything he does is grounded in reason. God does nothing by caprice.[32] And since God is all-powerful and controls all aspects of the universe, it follows that nothing in the world occurs through mere chance. For every event in the world, there corresponds a cause, and this cause is nothing other than God's reason for bringing this event—and not some other event—into being. Leibniz called this "the principle of sufficient reason." Voltaire, who rejected this principle, mentions it no fewer than seven times in *Candide*. Essentially, the principle of sufficient reason means that we do not fully understand something until we perceive why the thing is *exactly* the way it is—why God created it in its given form as opposed to some other form.

Consider Newtonian science, which Leibniz studied with great interest but did not consider real science. Newton was able to formulate the law of gravity according to which every thing in the universe attracts other things with a force that is proportional to the product of their masses and inversely proportional to the square of the distance between them. Newton was confident that his theory was sound because experiments verified it. But Leibniz's conception of science was based on a more demanding standard. He criticized Newton for merely *describing* the manner in which bodies are attracted to each other and not *explaining* why they are attracted to each other the way they are. For example, why is gravity inversely proportional to the *square* of the distance, instead of being inversely proportional to the *cube* of the distance?

[31]G. W. Leibniz, *Theodicy* (La Salle, Ill.: Open Court, 1985), 51, 53. First published in 1710, this book was the only one published in Leibniz's lifetime. Most of his work took the form of journal articles, unpublished memoranda, and letters.

[32]Ibid., 74.

Newton modestly admitted that he could not explain why the laws of nature are what they are, and he doubted that any ultimate reason could ever be found. Leibniz, in contrast, insisted that to honor God's intelligence we must search for the ultimate reason for the laws governing the world. We must recognize, in other words, that God selected the blueprint for the world out of a range of possible blueprints. And since God is rational, he must have selected this blueprint because it is best. Hence, it is part of the philosopher's job to show that the world has an optimal structure—that every phenomenon fits into a plan for "the best among all possible worlds."[33]

That is exactly what Voltaire refused to do. Throughout most of his life he was suspicious of grand philosophical systems that tried to explain the necessary connections among all things. He was an empiricist, which is to say that he admired scientists such as Newton, who made precise observations through experimentation and who generalized on the basis of these observations. He considered science valuable because it could be put to practical use, not because it answered every question about the essential nature of reality. In *Candide,* the brilliant sections on Eldorado (Chapters 17–18) portray an imaginary ideal country. There are no theologians and no metaphysicians in Eldorado, but there are many scientists and engineers who build machines that are useful for the people.

As for metaphysics, Voltaire described it as "an immense abyss in which everyone is blind."[34] Yet, Voltaire's position was inconsistent in the 1730s and 1740s, the period in which he was living with Madame du Châtelet, his mistress, who was a great admirer of Leibniz. Under her influence Voltaire sometimes leaned toward Leibniz's belief that everything in the world is arranged as it should be. But two events pushed him away from Leibniz once and for all. The first was Madame du Châtelet's death in 1749, which Voltaire could in no way construe as necessary and beneficial. By dying prematurely and for no evident good, Voltaire's mistress contradicted her own optimism, leaving Voltaire alone to scrutinize the reasons for unnecessary suffering in the world.

The second event was the great Lisbon earthquake of November 1, 1755. This disaster claimed the lives of tens of thousands of victims. Voltaire, overwhelmed by reports of innocent children crushed beneath the rubble, responded with a cry of protest against the assumption that a good God directs everything in the world for the best. In December he wrote a poem about the disaster and boldly questioned the belief that

[33]Ibid., 128; see also 138.
[34]Letter to Des Alleurs, 26 Nov. 1738; *Correspondence*, 89:378.

there is a moral purpose inherent in the universe.[35] Voltaire still believed in God, but he was now convinced that God had not arranged everything according to an ideal blueprint. He concluded that God is simply not as powerful as most people think—not strong enough to prevent evil.[36] This "shattered sense of cosmic security," as Henry calls it, is precisely what Barthes failed to detect in Voltaire's writings.[37] In *Candide,* written three years after the Lisbon earthquake, Voltaire expresses his permanent despondency by devoting a whole section (Chapter 5) to the disaster.

In fact, Voltaire ridicules Leibniz's cosmic optimism throughout *Candide.* The main vehicle of his satire is Pangloss, one of the most famous characters in modern literature. Pangloss is an expert in "metaphysico-theologico-cosmolo-boobology." With this term Voltaire pokes fun at Leibniz's all-encompassing philosophy. Pangloss, whose name means all-tongue, asserts that the world could not be better than it is because "all is for the best." He is always ready with a long-winded theory to explain that an apparent evil is really a good—even when it is obvious to everyone else that a disaster has occurred with no benefits for anyone. Pangloss is so out of touch, so obsessed with philosophical abstractions, that he is unable to give voice to anybody's pain, including his own. When he contracts a dreaded disease, all he can do is affirm—without really believing it—that his grotesque condition must be part of a system that works for the general good. Through Pangloss, Voltaire shows how stubborn people can be in their blindness to reality.

Scholars have sometimes argued that Pangloss is an unfair caricature of Leibniz, who, after all, was no fool.[38] They have suggested that Voltaire had only a superficial knowledge of Leibniz's thought and that his satire is not effective against Leibniz himself but only against the watered-down version of Leibniz's philosophy that one finds in books by his student Christian Wolff and in the poetry of Alexander Pope. In his *Essay on Man* (1733–34), Pope declared:

> All nature is but art, unknown to thee;
> All chance, direction which thou canst not see;
> All discord, harmony not understood;

[35]The full title of the poem is "Poem on the Lisbon Disaster, or Examination of That Axiom: 'All is Well.' "

[36]For an interesting discussion of Voltaire's view that God is not all-powerful, see A. J. Ayer, *Voltaire* (London: Weidenfeld and Nicolson, 1986), 118ff.

[37]Patrick Henry, "Contre Barthes," 29.

[38]John Weightman gives a good summary of this argument, "The Quality of *Candide,*" in *Essays Presented to C. M Girdlestone* (Newcastle upon Tyne: Durham University Press, 1960), 336–37.

All partial evil, universal good:
And, spite of pride, in erring reason's spite,
One truth is clear, Whatever is, is right.

Voltaire was certainly out to refute the simple optimism of Wolff and Pope. But he was also refuting Leibniz, whose philosophy he understood very well.

Voltaire did not respond to all the nuances of Leibniz's metaphysics, but he seized with great clarity its fundamental contradictions. One of the problems Leibniz never fully overcame was how to make sense of contingencies—in other words, how to explain events in the natural or human world that seem to occur by chance or to have no special significance. Consider the fact that an old man named John Doe died at 10:02 A.M. It would appear that the exact time of the death has no necessary relationship to any essential conception of who John Doe was as a person. In other words, we can imagine him dying at 10:03 or 10:01, and it would not change our image of him. But Leibniz maintained that everything that happens *must* happen, given the nature of the person or thing that it happens to. He affirmed that all apparent contingencies can be deduced logically from our fundamental knowledge of the subject. This means that someone who knew John Doe well when he was alive as a young man should have been able to deduce his precise time of death![39]

But this is clearly a very difficult position to sustain, and Leibniz knew it. He modified his theory several times and admitted that it was practically impossible for human beings to explain why every event takes place as it does. He continued to assert, however, that in principle nothing occurs through chance. God has arranged every detail of the world for a purpose. If we fail to detect this purpose, if we are unable to apply the principle of sufficient reason in practice, it is simply because our minds are not powerful enough to view the world from God's perspective.

Voltaire perceived this weakness and used it effectively to criticize Leibniz. In *Candide* he makes it clear that sometimes unpleasant things happen to people for reasons that are not a consequence of their own being. Misfortunes cannot be deduced logically from the qualities of the person they destroy. They simply result from the chaotic intersection of events. Thus, when a woman is raped and killed by soldiers in *Candide,* it is not due to her intrinsic nature or to a blueprint for a perfect

---

[39] Here I have attempted to summarize in untechnical language Leibniz's claim that all attributes of a thing are logically internal to it. For fuller discussion, see G. H. R. Parkinson, "Philosophy and Logic," in *The Cambridge Companion to Leibniz,* ed. Nicholas Jolley (Cambridge: Cambridge University Press, 1995), 199–223.

universe—it is due to the fact that she happens to be caught in the middle of a war. Leibniz ran into a similar difficulty in defending his view that God created "the best among all possible worlds." He recognized that misfortunes do occur, but he claimed that God allowed them to happen only as part of a process of creating a greater good.[40] But Leibniz admitted that it is sometimes very difficult for us to grasp how a specific evil is connected to a greater good. He affirmed, once again, that only God is in a position to perceive all the redeeming features of the world he created. Our duty is simply to trust that if we fully understood God's supreme wisdom, we would wish the world to be exactly as it is.[41]

Thus, on two separate points—the issue of contingency and the issue of evil—Leibniz backed into passive religious belief. His assertion that God does everything for a rational purpose begins as the premise of his system and ends as an article of faith which he uses to patch over the system's problems. Voltaire refused to enter this circle of faith—where faith means the idealization of reality. Even though both Leibniz and Voltaire believed in God and both were decent human beings, their temperaments were different. Leibniz loved God more than humankind, while Voltaire loved humankind more than God. Leibniz's whole system is, as he described it, "a vindication of [God's] perfections."[42] Voltaire's thought flowed from his sympathy for those who suffer. His particular brand of faith was that of a reformer who believed that even though God created the world, it might be possible to improve a bit upon His creation.

Voltaire thought Leibniz's ideas were not only logically unsound but also evil when put into practice. Precious time is wasted theorizing about the ultimate causes of things, time that could be better used reacting directly to events around us. When Candide is about to jump into the sea to save a drowning man, he is distracted from doing so by Pangloss, who theorizes on the necessity of the man's death. Voltaire is saying that when we engage in metaphysical philosophy, we ignore the passage of time and miss unique opportunities to intervene in history. While we theorize, we lose sight of reality, until reality makes us notice it by afflicting us with the very same misfortunes that we trivialized when they afflicted others. In *Candide,* Voltaire expresses this rather heavy insight with a light touch: whenever the characters immerse themselves in theory, they never move forward in their conclusions. Meanwhile, the world around them always changes, whether they notice it or not. For example:

[40]Leibniz, *Theodicy,* 128–29.
[41]Ibid., 55.
[42]Ibid., 61.

While he was perfecting his logical proof, the ship broke into two and everyone perished . . .

When one of the characters wisely concludes in the last chapter, "Let us work without theorizing," it is the last point in Voltaire's denunciation of Leibniz.

Now the reason that Voltaire stopped writing philosophical treatises and began writing stories like *Candide* should be clear. Philosophers had failed to explain why human beings suffer. Voltaire came to the conclusion that there is in fact no overarching explanation. The point is not to account for evil logically but to narrate it vividly. For Voltaire the purpose of literature (and also history, which he wrote a lot of) is to represent the amazing incidents of the world in the only way they can be represented: as a series of events that did not have to happen but did in fact happen. He does not seek to rationalize reality; he only seeks to tell tales that make us face it.

Ridicule, Sex, Irony

But there is another reason that Voltaire liked to write stories more than philosophical treatises: he wanted to be funny! *Candide* is soaked with suffering, yet it is buoyant with humor. It is a tragicomedy in which we laugh our way to a sober understanding of the world. Voltaire knew many ways to make people smile. One of them is *ridicule*—the act of singling out someone for witty and merciless criticism. Voltaire's ridicule could be indignant, especially against anyone who denied his own greatness. In 1759 when *Candide* was published, a journalist named Elie Fréron wrote a review of it. Fréron was an enemy of Voltaire and the Enlightenment. He edited a publication called *L'Année littéraire* (The Literary Year); Voltaire liked to call it *L'Âne littéraire* (The Literary Ass). In his review, Fréron sarcastically pretended that *Candide* was a horrible book and that someone as distinguished as Voltaire could not possibly have written it. (Fréron's review appears in the related documents in this volume.) Voltaire answered by modifying *Candide* for the 1761 edition so as to include Fréron in the story. In this new section, located in Chapter 22, Candide attends a play that he enjoys. In fact, it is one of Voltaire's own plays that Candide sees! A pseudosophisticated art critic informs him that the play is worthless. Afterwards Candide asks his companion, "Who was that fat pig?" and his companion responds that it is a stupid writer "who makes a living by saying nasty things about every play and every book." And he adds the devastating words, "He hates anyone who becomes popular, just as eunuchs hate anyone who makes love." A few lines later, the impotent "fat pig" is identified as Fréron.

This example of ridicule shows another aspect of Voltaire's style: his sexual playfulness. Sex is everywhere in the book. It should be no surprise, for many Enlightenment authors, seeking to capture a broad audience and to influence the thinking of ordinary people, infused their works with sexual themes.[43] Yet, readers today often assume that people in the eighteenth century must have been more reserved, more prudish than we are today. It might not occur to us that Voltaire was as shocking as anything we encounter in today's culture. We run the risk of not registering his innuendo because, when we run into a passage that sounds like it might be about sex, we say to ourselves, "Oh no, he couldn't mean *that!*" But innuendo, or the art of suggesting something outrageous without saying it explicitly, is one of Voltaire's great techniques of humor. The book is filled with these understated outrages, and they are very often of a sexual kind. Here is an example.

In Chapter 10, Candide, his lover Cunégonde, and their servant, who is called "the old woman," are at an inn. They are fleeing from the police because Candide has killed two men. Cunégonde and the female servant share a room. When Cunégonde rises in the morning, she finds that someone has stolen her money and jewels. The old woman suspects that the thief was a Franciscan monk who, she says, "came into our chamber twice" during the night. The reader naturally wonders why the old woman is volunteering this information so late. Why didn't she say anything when she saw the monk enter their room? There is no explicit answer in the chapters, but here is the answer suggested by innuendo. "Came into our chamber twice" is a double-entendre: Voltaire is saying that the old woman copulated with the monk, not just once but twice. That is why she kept quiet. The innuendo is outrageous because monks are supposed to be celibate. Voltaire took delight in showing the hypocrisy of the clergy. But it is even more outrageous because the old woman is so old and because she is horribly ugly: her nose touches her chin, and she is missing one buttock.

A reserved reader might suspect that this interpretation goes too far. But how else to explain the fact that the old woman watched a monk enter her room during the night and did not say anything? Besides, Voltaire often clarifies his innuendo in subsequent chapters. In other words, he drops a hint in one place and confirms the most outrageous implications

---

[43]Robert Darnton, *The Forbidden Best-Sellers of Pre-Revolutionary France* (New York: W. W. Norton, 1995).

afterward with a second hint. The same monk is mentioned a few chapters later; this time he is described as "a long-sleeved Franciscan." It is a fairly natural term to use, because long sleeves were part of the clothing of the Franciscan order. But the word for sleeve in French is *manche,* and this word also meant shaft, handle, or tube. We are back in the realm of sexual innuendo again, and the lewd overtones confirm our reading of the earlier scene.

The same pattern occurs many times in the tale: a subtle hint of unconventional sexual action is followed by other hints so that we do not miss the allusion. In this way, Voltaire is able to portray certain relationships with a very subtle mockery. But sometimes the mockery is so nuanced that we suspect Voltaire is sympathizing with the victim of his own sarcasm and we are thrown off guard. The complicated theme of homosexuality is a case in point.

In Chapter 2, when Candide is recruited against his will into the army of the "Bulgars," various details of the scene make it clear that the Bulgars symbolize the Prussians under Frederick II. As many commentators have noted, the word "Bulgar" also sounds like the French word *bougre* (bugger), which means a sodomite or homosexual. (In fact, *bougre* is etymologically derived from the Latin *bulgarus,* a term used in the late Middle Ages to refer to heretics in Eastern Europe who allegedly engaged in homosexuality.) The reader's suspicion that Voltaire is deriding Frederick by implying that he is a homosexual is confirmed by other words in the text. The King of the Bulgars is described as "charming" and the other soldiers encourage Candide to feel a "tender" love for him. In a later chapter, it is mentioned—almost in passing—that Cunégonde's brother was raped by Bulgar soldiers. It seems that Voltaire saw homosexuality as a deviation from normality and that the whole point of portraying Frederick and his soldiers as homosexuals was to condemn them. France was at war with Prussia when Voltaire wrote *Candide,* so the homosexuality theme appears to be good propaganda against the enemy.

It is not so simple. Voltaire clearly wished to deflate the majestic image of Frederick II, known as Frederick the Great. Portraying Frederick and his subjects as homosexuals helped him to cut the famous Prussian down to size. However, nothing in Voltaire's writings suggests that he was outraged by homosexual behavior. In his *Philosophical Dictionary* there is an entry entitled "So-Called Socratic Love." Here Voltaire noted that it was common for men to have a passion for other men and he described this passion as "natural."[44] He did not go so far as to endorse sodomy, but nei-

---

[44]For fuller discussion see Michel Delon, "The Priest, the Philosopher, and Homosexuality in Enlightenment France," in *'Tis Nature's Fault: Unauthorized Sexuality during the*

ther did he endorse its legal repression. Several other thinkers of the Enlightenment went so far as to call for the complete decriminalization of homosexuality. Even the religious and political authorities accepted that homosexual relations were widespread. Officially, homosexual activity was a serious offense punishable by death; but in practice, such activity was widely tolerated, especially in the upper classes. Those who were arrested usually got off with light penalties.[45]

But there is more: Voltaire and Frederick were deeply attached to each other. They began to correspond in 1736. The Prussian prince was then only twenty-four and still under the cruel supervision of his militaristic father, Frederick William I. Frederick eventually emerged as a superb military leader in his own right, but only after his father's death. As a young man he sought to escape the iron discipline. He played the flute and wrote poetry. Frederick William despised his son's "feminine" tastes and regularly humiliated him. When Frederick initiated the correspondence with Voltaire, he was searching for a softer, more refined mentor. This correspondence, consisting of more than seven hundred letters, lasted until 1778, the year of Voltaire's death. Despite periods of mutual hostility, it was an affectionate and enduring bond. Haydn Mason, a very careful scholar, has presented evidence to suggest that Voltaire consummated his love for Frederick during his stay at the Prussian court in 1740.[46] Whatever the precise nature of their physical relationship, there is no doubt that Voltaire was strongly attracted to Frederick. In a letter of 1751 to the Duc de Richelieu, Voltaire described how he had been enchanted instantly by Frederick's "large blue eyes and gentle smile." He found his "head swirling" in the presence of Frederick's "seductive" gestures. "I gave myself to him with passion, with blindness, and without reasoning," he added.[47]

Thus, while Voltaire poked fun at other people's homosexual activity, he was aware of his own sexual ambivalence. His jokes, which begin in mockery, end in surprising self-disclosure. In *Candide,* he brilliantly turns this problem of the unpredictability of desire into a commentary not on homosexuals but on the whole human race. Candide is on a quest to find Cunégonde and marry her. He is like the hero of Homer's *Odyssey* who longs to return home from war to be with his faithful love. But Candide

---

Enlightenment, ed. Robert Maccubbin (Cambridge: Cambridge University Press, 1987), 124–25.

[45]Delon, 122–23; and Bryant T. Ragan, "The Enlightenment Confronts Homosexuality," in *Homosexuality in Modern France,* ed. Jeffrey Merrick and Bryant T. Ragan (New York: Oxford University Press, 1996), 8–29.

[46]Mason, *Voltaire,* 52–54.

[47]Voltaire, letter of 31 Aug., 1751, in *Correspondence,* 96:273–74.

is sidetracked. He has at least two affairs before he finds Cunégonde, one of them with a man.[48] And when he is finally reunited with the woman of his dreams, what he finds bears no resemblance to what he was seeking. Possession of her turns out to be as much a problem as separation had been. *Candide* is not a Homeric epic but a mockery of what the epic stands for: unswerving loyalty to a manly cause that rewards those who persevere.

In short, Voltaire believed that no one lives life with perfect consistency. That is another reason why he preferred to write stories rather than develop his ideas in philosophical treatises. The assumption underlying philosophy is that ideas and actions should unfold without contradiction. Voltaire's starting point is that humans are inherently contradictory. Since logic cannot represent human nature, a different style of writing is needed. Ridicule and innuendo are part of this style, but the crucial element is *irony*.

Broadly speaking, there are two kinds of irony: irony of plot and irony of language. Irony of plot is a series of events that ends in a totally unexpected manner: the "good guy" turns out to be the "bad guy," the slow person wins the race. Voltaire uses irony in this way, but the extraordinary cleverness of *Candide* has more to do with the other kind. Irony of language is a paragraph, a sentence, or even a phrase that turns out to have a meaning that is the opposite of the one it seemed to have in the beginning. In Chapter 1, Voltaire begins a paragraph with, "The Baron was one of the most powerful lords . . . , " but by the end of the paragraph we see that the Baron is a provincial nobody. Examples of irony within a single sentence occur throughout the book. Consider this one:

> The beautiful lady had observed two enormous diamonds on the fingers of her young visitor, and she praised them so unselfishly that they passed from Candide's fingers to hers.

Here the irony springs from the word "unselfishly." By the end of the sentence above, it is clear that the lady wants the rings for herself; she pretends to be kind only to trick the innocent Candide into responding with a kindness of his own.

Voltaire is the master of compressed irony in which words rapidly contradict the meaning of previous words. Often he does not need a full sen-

---

[48]No other commentator, I believe, has noted the innuendo with which Voltaire situates Candide in a homosexual relationship with a priest called "the Perigordian Abbé." My interpretation rests on some technical semantic considerations. See the "Note on Voltaire's Vocabulary and the Present Translation."

tence to create the effect of irony. He simply relies on brilliant oxymorons, that is, incongruous or self-contradictory phrases. For example, when he describes a battle as "heroic," the reader thinks for a second that he admires the fight. But the very next word turns the description into a paradox: it is "heroic butchery." The surprising pairing of opposites forces the reader to think about the brutal reality that accompanies grand military rhetoric.

For Voltaire, irony is a philosophical antimethod that forces the reader to question the integrity of every character and the consistency of every moral in the story that he tells. Very little gets past Voltaire's implacable negativism. It is understandable why the Romantic novelist Bernardin de Saint-Pierre stated, "Voltaire is concerned with little else than to destroy."[49] But *Candide* also moves beyond cynicism. By the end, the principal characters have gained some wisdom and they manage to forge a life of honest work. The lesson that emerges in the conclusion of *Candide* is *Il faut cultiver notre jardin:* We must cultivate our garden.

The meaning of this famous line is by no means clear-cut. It is one of those immortal sayings that relates nothing in particular but simply conveys a wise reconciliation with the hardships of life. There is room to interpret each word in different ways. But whatever it may mean to "cultivate" a good life, Voltaire makes it clear that it must be different from living like Pangloss, a theorist who builds empty arguments and learns nothing through the passage of time. And whatever it may mean to work in the "garden," it surely cannot be a return to the Garden of Eden, where people lived in innocence, with all their desires gratified, prior to God's imposition of suffering on humankind. The garden in *Candide* symbolizes whatever life the individual is able to salvage *after* a long process of suffering.

With his combination of scathing criticism and modest hope, Voltaire managed to produce a work of great popularity. When it was first published in 1759, a spokesman for the Parlement of Paris, the highest law court in France, denounced it as "contrary to religion and good morals."[50] (The full text is in the related documents section.) An assembly of ministers in Geneva condemned it for "containing dirty things . . . contrary to good morals and injurious to Providence."[51] But the reading public

---

[49]Cited in Raymond Naves, "Voltaire's Wisdom," *Voltaire: A Collection of Critical Essays,* ed. William F. Bottiglia (Englewood Cliffs, N. J.: Prentice-Hall, 1968), 151.

[50]Omer Joly de Fleury to Henry-Léonard-Jean-Baptiste Bertin, 24 Feb. 1759; *Correspondence,* 103:426.

[51]See appendix 173, "Candide before the Genevese authorities, February 1759," in *Correspondence,* 103:449.

loved it. Over twenty thousand copies were sold within a year in Paris, Geneva, Amsterdam, London, and other major European cities. By the standards of the eighteenth century, it was a best seller. It went on to become a classic. It has been translated into dozens of languages, including Ukrainian, Chinese, and Arabic. Today it is one of the three or four most widely known books by a French author.

Since this Bedford/St. Martin's edition has been prepared especially for university students, it is worth noting that Voltaire, in his sixties, composed a tale well suited for readers younger than himself. The story of a teenage boy and girl who dream of happiness but who must confront a world where even God is not strong enough to prevent misfortune—such a story seems designed for those who are still immersed in doubts rather than those who have settled into dogmatic certainty. After years of examinations, students might find refreshment in a book that is a summary of problems that are not meant to be solved. From Voltaire, the outspoken reformer and philosophical skeptic, one can learn that it is possible to act without pretending to know all the answers. He represents a middle way between the fanatical self-assurance and dazed passivity that increasingly divide the world in which we live.

NOTE ON VOLTAIRE'S VOCABULARY AND THE PRESENT TRANSLATION

Candide was first published in 1759. The 1775 edition, printed in Geneva by Cramer and Bardin, was the last edition published before Voltaire's death and under his editorial control. In his critical French edition of *Candide,* René Pomeau used the 1775 edition, and I have used Pomeau's text as the basis for the present translation.[1] For most of the related documents at the end of this volume, I have relied on Theodore Besterman's definitive *Correspondence and Related Documents* in *The Complete Works of Voltaire* (Geneva: Institut et Musée Voltaire, 1968–77). I am grateful to the Voltaire Foundation at Oxford University for permission to translate these superbly edited texts.

Several English translations of *Candide* already exist, so something should be said about the principles underlying this new one: accuracy, appreciation of innuendo, and readability.

Accuracy

I have consulted modern dictionaries based on historical principles as well as dictionaries from the eighteenth century. Some improvements in the rendering of particular words have resulted. When Candide enters an inn in Eldorado (Chapter 17), he is asked to be seated at the *table de l'hôte,* which is usually translated as "the host's table." This implies that he is honored as a special guest. But as eighteenth-century dictionaries reveal, *table de l'hôte* meant the common table, and the point is that in Eldorado there are no distinctions: everyone sits together as equals.

In Chapter 2, when Candide is recruited into the Bulgar army because of his height, we are told that his height is *cinq pieds cinq pouces*—which all previous translations give as five feet five inches. This is a surprising figure considering that the Bulgars symbolize the Prussians, who were known for their tall soldiers, and five feet five inches was not particularly tall, even in the eighteenth century when people were generally shorter than they are today. The mystery is solved when we take into account that a *pied du roi* under the Old Regime was .324 meters, considerably more than an English foot. Candide's real height is between five feet ten and five feet eleven inches. René Pomeau already signaled this fact in his critical edition, but none of the English translators appear to have profited from Pomeau's useful notes. If nothing else, the present translation can claim to restore Candide to his true stature!

---

[1]*Candide ou l'optimisme, édition critique par René Pomeau* (Oxford: The Voltaire Foundation, 1980).

Innuendo

The meaning of expressions such as *table de l'hôte* and *pied* can be ascertained by consulting external reference works, such as old dictionaries. The meaning of some words, however, is grounded inside the text. That is, Voltaire generates meaning by instituting semantic overtones within the book that do not inhere in basic dictionary definitions. An important example is the expression *faire les honneurs* (literally, "to do the honors" but translated in this volume as "to bestow favors on"). In French, as in English, this expression is highly elastic and can be used in a variety of situations in which one person makes a gracious gesture to another. Voltaire, however, wreaks havoc with the term by using it ironically to refer to sex. Recounting her youth, the old woman states (Chapter 11):

> I was ravishing, I was beauty and grace made flesh, and I was a virgin. But not for long. The flower I had reserved for the handsome prince of Massa-Carrara was plucked by the pirate captain . . . who thought he was bestowing great favors on me *(me faire beaucoup d'honneur)*.

Later, in Chapter 22, a worldly Marquise says to Candide, "I sometimes force my Parisian lovers to languish for two weeks, but I am giving myself to you on the first night, because one should always bestow the favors *(faire les honneurs)* of one's country on a young man from Westphalia."

Now, what are we to make of the line, also in Chapter 22, which says that a Perigordian Abbé "bestowed favors" *(faisaient les honneurs)* upon Candide? Here there is no obvious sexual connotation within the sentence, but the other usages of the term create an inevitable echo effect. Voltaire is hinting that Candide has a homosexual relationship with the Abbé. Two chapters later, he confirms the hint. Candide laments that he has been looking for Cunégonde for many months without finding her. "All I've encountered in her place," he says, "is one pretentious strumpet and one Perigordian Abbé." Since there is no doubt about Candide's affair with the Marquise (referred to here as the "strumpet"), this line is conclusive.

The point is that if one were to underestimate Voltaire's erotic imagination and neglect the semantic web that he spins over the course of the tale, one would miss several bold features of the story. Throughout the translation, I have made an effort to transmit Voltaire's outrageous wit, which earlier translators have obtusely erased. For example, by translating *faire les honneurs* as "to bestow favors," I have made the verb slightly more aggressive and the noun slightly more suggestive than in the vacuous literal rendering, "to do the honors."

It should be added that the process of tracking the inflection of particular words throughout a text has relevance beyond the reconstruction of sexual innuendo. An important example is the verb *raisonner,* usually translated with the cognate "to reason." When Voltaire uses this verb in *Candide,* however, he is generally referring to a particular type of reasoning: the grand metaphysical theorizing of people who believe they can understand the ultimate causes of all things. When Martin says, in a crucial line, *"Travaillons sans raisonner,"* he speaks for Voltaire. He is not saying "Let us work without reasoning," which implies anti-intellectualism. He is saying that it is futile to try to preface all our endeavors with abstract justifications. We must keep thinking, but we must also be willing to act even in the absence of intellectual certainty. Hence, a better translation is, "Let us work without theorizing."[2]

Readability

Voltaire intended his *contes,* or short novels, to be read and understood by a broad audience. "Could one not write a book that might be read with some pleasure, by the very people who do not like to read, a book which might bring hearts to compassion?"[3] An excessive reliance on cognates is one fault that can ruin the simplicity of a translation and has in fact done so in many English versions of *Candide.* For while the English–French cognate may have the same meaning in each language, it may be a very ordinary word in French and a rare one in English. One can end up transforming colloquial French into pretentious English in this way.

In reading through other English translations, I often came across many English words that I did not understand and that reduced my comprehension of the text. In this translation, I have kept the vocabulary simple because that is how the original is. I have said "whip" where some translators have said "pizzle," "cent" instead of "sou," and so forth. I also do not see the point of using an obscure English word and clarifying it for the reader with a footnote when Voltaire selected French words that would be recognizable to his readers.

Robert M. Adams, the translator of the Norton edition of *Candide,* deserves credit for preserving respect for English idiom. His colloquialisms sometimes strike me as more British than American, but it is a pleasure to acknowledge a distinguished predecessor who has influenced some of my decisions.

---

[2]On this point I follow Patrick Henry, "Raisonner in *Candide," Romanic Review* 80 (1980), 362–70.
[3]Voltaire to Moulton, Oct./Nov. 1766; *Correspondence,* 115:58.

Voltaire at 41 years of age, painted by Maurice Quentin de La Tour.

Above: Woodcut showing Voltaire reading to Frederick the Great of Prussia in the garden of Sans-Souci, Frederick's chateau. Voltaire lived at Frederick's court from 1750 to 1753. *Left:* A sculpture of the elderly Voltaire by Jean-Antoine Houdon, 1780.

Madame du Châtelet, Voltaire's companion and collaborator for sixteen years, by a painter of the French school.

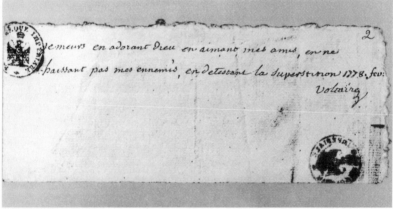

Top: A bust of Voltaire being crowned at the Théâtre Français, March 30, 1778.
Bottom: Voltaire's declaration of faith, February 28, 1778: "I die worshipping God, loving my friends, not hating my enemies, detesting superstition."
Right: Illustration from 1787 edition of *Candide* showing the scene in which Candide encounters an African slave. The mutilated slave says, "It is at this price that you eat sugar in Europe."

C'eſt à ce prix que vous mangez du ſucre
en Europe.

Candide Chapitre 19

J. M. Moreau le j.ᵉⁿ 1787 Baquoy filius Sculp.

PART TWO

Candide,

or Optimism

Translated from the German of Dr. Ralph. With the Additions Found in the Doctor's Pocket When He Died at Minden in the Year of Our Lord 1759[1]

CHAPTER 1

How Candide was brought up in a fine castle, and how he was driven out of it

In the land of Westphalia, in the castle of the Baron of Thunder-ten-tronckh, lived a youth endowed by nature with the gentlest of characters. His face was the mirror of his soul. His judgment was quite sound, his mind simple as could be; this is the reason, I think, that he was named Candide. The old servants of the house suspected that he was the son of the Baron's sister and of a good and honorable gentleman of the region whom that lady refused to marry because he could prove only seventy-one generations of noble lineage, the rest of his family tree having been lost in the shadows of time.

The Baron was one of the most powerful lords in Westphalia because his castle had a gate and windows. His reception hall was even decorated with a piece of tapestry. The barnyard dogs formed a hunting pack when

---

[1]Voltaire denied authorship to protect himself from punishment. The use of a patently false pseudonym also creates an atmosphere of playfulness and encourages the reader to be skeptical.

Minden is a Westphalian town where one of the great battles of the Seven Years' War (1756–63) took place. In Chapter 3, Voltaire portrays this war in which France, Austria, Sweden, and Russia were aligned on one side against Prussia and Great Britain.

the need arose; the stable boys doubled as his attendants in the chase; the village vicar was his archpriest. They all called him My Lord, and they always laughed at his jokes.

The Baroness, who weighed around three hundred and fifty pounds, was widely admired for that reason, and bestowed favors on visitors with a discretion that made her even more eminent. Her daughter Cunégonde, aged seventeen, was rosy-cheeked, fresh, plump, and appetizing. The Baron's son seemed to be the equal of his father in every way. The tutor Pangloss was the oracle of the household, and little Candide absorbed his lessons with all the good faith of his age and character.

Pangloss taught metaphysico-theologico-cosmolo-boobology.[2] He proved admirably that there is no effect without a cause and that, in this best of all possible worlds, the Baron's castle was the finest of all castles, and his wife the best of all possible Baronesses.[3]

"It has been proven," he used to say, "that things cannot be other than what they are, for since everything is made for an end, everything is necessarily for the best end. Observe that noses were made to wear spectacles, hence we have spectacles. Legs are patently devised to be breeched, and so we have breeches. Stones were made to be quarried and to build castles with; hence My Lord has a fine castle. The greatest Baron of the province must have the finest residence. And since pigs were made to be eaten, we eat pork all year round. Therefore, those who have affirmed that all is well talk nonsense; they ought to have said that all is for the best."[4]

Candide listened attentively and believed innocently; for he found Miss Cunégonde extremely beautiful, though he never dared to tell her so. He concluded that after the happiness of being born Baron of Thunder-ten-tronckh, the second degree of happiness was to be Miss Cunégonde, the third was to see her every day, and the fourth was to listen to Master Pangloss, the greatest philosopher in the province and consequently in the whole world.

One day, as Cunégonde was strolling near the castle in the tiny woods they called the Park, she saw Dr. Pangloss in the bushes giving a lesson

---

[2] I have inserted "boob" into this comical word because the French contains "nigo," the phonetic equivalent of *nigaud* (boob).

[3] The principle that every effect has a cause or rational explanation, and the phrase "best of all possible worlds," come from the German philosopher Gottfried Wilhelm Leibniz (1646–1716). See the introduction for a fuller discussion of Leibniz.

[4] The name Pangloss means all-tongue. Here he expounds his optimistic philosophy — that everything in the world exists for a good purpose. In this paragraph, as throughout the story, Pangloss uses logical connectives (such as "for" and "therefore") to link statements that in fact have no logical relationship.

in experimental physics to her mother's maid, a very cute and obedient brunette. Now Miss Cunégonde was very intrigued by the sciences. She observed breathlessly the repeated experiments performed before her eyes. She saw clearly the doctor's sufficient reason and the action of cause and effect. And she turned back to the house all excited, all distracted, all consumed by the desire to become more instructed in science, dreaming that she might be young Candide's sufficient reason—and that he might be hers.

She met Candide on the way back to the castle. She blushed, and so did he. She said hello in a faltering voice, and Candide replied without knowing what he was saying. The next day, when they left the table after dinner, Cunégonde and Candide found themselves behind a partition. Cunégonde dropped her handkerchief, Candide picked it up. She innocently took his hand, the young man innocently kissed it with remarkable animation, emotion, and grace. Their lips met, their eyes glowed, their knees trembled, their hands wandered. The Baron of Thunder-ten-tronck came around the partition and, seeing this cause and this effect, drove Candide out of the castle with great kicks in the behind. Cunégonde fainted. As soon as she recovered, the Baroness slapped her face, and everything was unsettled in this finest and most agreeable of all possible castles.

CHAPTER 2

What became of Candide among the Bulgars

Expelled from earthly paradise, Candide walked for a long time without knowing where he was going, weeping, raising his eyes to heaven, and looking back frequently toward the finest of castles which contained the most lovely of baron's daughters. He lay down to sleep, without supper, in the furrow of a plowed field. The snow came down in large flakes. The next day, chilled to the bone, Candide dragged himself toward the nearest town, called Waldberghoff-trarbk-dikdorff. Penniless and dying of hunger and exhaustion, he came to a sad halt at the door of an inn. Two men dressed in blue noticed him.

"Comrade," said one of them, "there is a well-built lad, and he is the right height too."

They approached Candide and politely invited him to dinner.

"Gentlemen," Candide answered with charming modesty, "you honor me greatly, but I lack the means to pay my share."

"But sir!" said one of the blues, "we never make people pay who have your looks and merit. Aren't you five feet ten inches tall?"[5]

"Yes, gentlemen, that's my height," he said with a bow.

"Then, sir, kindly be seated. We will not only pay for your dinner, but we will never let a man like you fall short of money. Men are created only in order to help each other."

"You're right," said Candide. "That's what Dr. Pangloss always told me, and I see clearly that everything is for the best."

They urged him to accept a little money. He took it and offered to sign a promissory note, but they would not hear of it, and they all sat down to eat.

"Don't you have a tender love for your . . . "

"Oh yes!" Candide answered. "I have a tender love for Miss Cunégonde."

"No," one of the men stated, "we want to know if you have a tender love for the King of the Bulgars."[6]

"Not at all," he said, "since I've never met him."

"What? He is the most charming of kings, and we must drink to his health."

"All right, I'll be happy to, gentlemen!" And he drank.

"That's enough," they said. "You are now the pillar, the upholder, the defender, the hero of the Bulgars: your fortune is made, and your glory assured."

Immediately they put irons on his feet and led him to the regiment. He had to turn right, turn left, order arms, load arms, aim, fire, and do it all in double time.[7] At the end he got thirty strokes of the rod. The next day, he did the drill a little less badly and got only twenty. The third day he got only ten, and was regarded by his comrades as a prodigy.

Candide, completely bewildered, did not yet discern very clearly how he was a hero. One fine spring day he took it into his head to go for a walk. He kept going forward, believing that humans, just like animals, had

---

[5]Frederick the Great took pride in the height of his soldiers. Other English translations make Candide's height five feet five inches. The error is based on a misunderstanding of the French word *pied,* which represented .324 meters before the French Revolution.

[6]The "Bulgars" is a thinly disguised term for the Prussians. Voltaire liked to insinuate that the Prussian leader, Frederick the Great, and his soldiers were sodomites. The French term *bougre* (bugger) not only sounds like *Bulgare* (translated in this chapter as Bulgar) but is etymologically derived from the Latin *bulgarus,* used in the late Middle Ages to refer to Eastern European heretics and sodomites.

[7]Frederick's army was famous for the speed with which it loaded and discharged firearms. In his *Histoire de la guerre de 1741,* Voltaire noted that the Prussian soldiers could shoot at least five times per minute.

the right to use their legs as they wished. He had barely gone five miles, when four other heroes, all over six feet, caught up with him, tied him, and threw him in a dungeon. In accordance with due process, he was asked which he preferred: to be thrashed thirty-six times by the entire regiment, or to receive twelve bullets in the brain all at once. He protested that human will is free and that he desired neither alternative; but he was forced to choose. Making use of the divine *liberty*[8] that still remained to him, he elected to run the gauntlet thirty-six times. Two times he did so. The regiment was made up of two thousand men. That made four thousand strokes of the rod, which laid bare every muscle and nerve from his neck to his behind. As they were preparing for the third run, Candide, unable to go on, requested them to be kind enough to smash in his head.

The request was granted. They blindfolded him and told him to kneel. At that moment the King of the Bulgars arrived on the scene and inquired about the victim's crime. Now the King was a genius and understood from what he was told that Candide was a young metaphysician, utterly ignorant about the things of this world, and he pardoned him with a generosity that will be praised in all newspapers and in all ages. A worthy surgeon cured Candide in three weeks with the ointments prescribed by Dioscorides.[9] He already had a little skin and was able to walk when the King of the Bulgars joined battle with the King of the Abars.[10]

CHAPTER 3

How Candide escaped from the Bulgars, and what became of him

Nothing was so splendid, so brisk, so brilliant, and so well-ordered as these two armies. The trumpets, fifes, oboes, drums, and cannons produced such a harmony as was never heard in hell. First the cannons laid low about six thousand men on each side; then the musketry removed from the best of worlds around nine or ten thousand scoundrels who were festering on its surface. The bayonet was also the sufficient reason for the death of several thousand men. The total must have been about thirty

[8]When he was younger Voltaire believed that God had granted to human beings the same liberty to do as they pleased that God himself possessed. By the time he wrote *Candide,* however, Voltaire appreciated that in many situations people have no effective range of choice; "liberty" in such circumstances is merely an empty word.
[9]A Greek physician who lived in the first century A.D.
[10]The Abars represent the French.

thousand souls. Candide, trembling like a philosopher, hid himself as best he could while this heroic butchery took place.

Finally, while each king was having his forces celebrate victory with a *Te Deum*,[11] Candide decided to theorize about causes and effects somewhere else. Making his way through heaps of the dead and dying, he came to a nearby village; it had been reduced to ashes. This was an Abar village that the Bulgars had burned in accordance with international law. Here, old men riddled with wounds looked on as life departed from their wives whose throats had been slit and whose children still clung to their blood-soaked breasts. There, young girls who had been disemboweled after they had satisfied the natural needs of various heroes, heaved their last sighs. Others, half-burned, screamed for someone to hasten their deaths. Brains were spattered over the ground amidst severed arms and legs.

Candide fled full speed to another village. This one belonged to the Bulgars, and the Abar heroes had treated it in the same manner. Forging onward through ruins and treading upon twitching limbs, Candide at last arrived outside the theater of war, carrying a few provisions in his knapsack and never forgetting Miss Cunégonde. His supplies ran out when he was in Holland; but having heard that everyone in this country was rich and that the people there were Christians, he had no doubt that he would be treated as well as he had been in the Baron's castle before he had been driven from it on account of the lovely eyes of Miss Cunégonde.

He requested alms of several grave individuals. They all replied that if he continued to beg he would be shut up in a house of correction to teach him how to behave.

Then he approached a man who had just finished giving a lecture on the topic of charity for a whole hour to a large assembly.[12] The orator looked askance at him and said:

"What are you doing here? Are you here for the good cause?"

"There is no effect without a cause," Candide answered modestly.[13] "Everything is linked by necessity and arranged for the best. I had to be driven from Miss Cunégonde; I had to run the gauntlet; and I have to beg for my bread until I can earn it. None of this could have been otherwise."

---

[11]A *Te Deum* is a prayer of thanks to God. After a military triumph, European monarchs often ordered their subjects to attend services and say the prayer.

[12]In other words, a Protestant minister.

[13]Candide assumes that the minister is using Pangloss's jargon when he utters the word "cause."

"My friend," said the orator, "do you believe the Pope is the Antichrist?"

"I never heard anyone say so," answered Candide, "but whether he is or not, I have no bread."

"And you do not deserve to eat any," said the other. "Go away, you scoundrel, you wretch, and never show your face here again!"

The orator's wife, having watched from a window above, and seeing a man who was not sure the Pope was the Antichrist, poured on his head a pot full of——. Oh Heavens! The zeal of pious women knows no bounds!

A man who had never been baptized, a good Anabaptist named Jacques,[14] saw the cruel and ignominious treatment inflicted on one of his fellows, a two-legged creature without feathers and with a soul. He took Candide home, washed him, gave him bread and beer, presented him with two florins, and even volunteered to teach him how to work in his Dutch factory, which specialized in the production of authentic Persian rugs. Candide was ready to kiss the man's feet and exclaimed:

"Dr. Pangloss was certainly right to tell me that all is for the best in this world. I am infinitely more touched by your extreme generosity than by the harshness of that gentleman in the black coat and his wife."

The next day, on a walk, he met a beggar all covered with sores, his eyes dull as death, the end of his nose rotting, mouth twisted, teeth black, a raspy voice, tortured by a violent cough, and spitting out a tooth with every spasm.

CHAPTER 4

How Candide met his old philosophy teacher, Dr. Pangloss, and what ensued

Candide, touched by horror and even more by compassion, gave this dreadful beggar the two florins he had received from Jacques, the worthy Anabaptist. The phantom stared at him, burst into tears, and threw his arms around his neck. Candide recoiled in terror.

"Alas," said one wretch to the other, "don't you recognize your dear Pangloss any more?"

"Can it be so? You, my dear master! You, in this horrible state! What

---

[14]The Anabaptists were Protestants who opposed infant baptism.

misfortune has befallen you? Why are you no longer in the finest of castles? What has become of Miss Cunégonde, that pearl of young ladies, that masterpiece of nature?"

"I cannot go on," said Pangloss.

Candide promptly led him to the Anabaptist's stable, where he gave him a morsel of bread, and when Pangloss had recovered:

"Well," said he, "Cunégonde?"

"She is dead," replied Pangloss.

Candide fainted at this word. His friend revived him with some old vinegar that happened to be in the stable. Candide opened his eyes.

"Cunégonde is dead! Ah, best of worlds, where are you now? But what illness did she die of? Did it stem from seeing me violently kicked out of her father's fine castle?"

"No," said Pangloss. "She was disemboweled by Bulgar soldiers after being raped until she was unconscious. They smashed in the head of the Baron when he tried to defend her; the Baroness was hacked to pieces; and my poor pupil was treated exactly the same as his sister. As for the castle, not one stone was left standing upright. Not a single barn, sheep, duck, or tree is left. But we have avenged ourselves in full, for the Abars did the same thing to a nearby estate that belonged to a Bulgar lord."

At this account Candide fainted again, but after he came back to his senses and expressed his sorrow, he inquired about the cause and effect, the sufficient reason, which had reduced Pangloss to such a pitiful state.

"Alas," said he, "it is love; love, the consoler of the human race, the guardian of the universe, the soul of all sensitive beings, tender love."

"Alas," said Candide, "I have known this love, this ruler of hearts, this soul of our soul: it never got me anything except one kiss and twenty kicks in the ass. And why did this beautiful cause produce in you such a disgusting effect?"

Pangloss answered in these terms:

"Oh my dear Candide! You knew Paquette, our venerable Baron's pretty maid. In her arms I tasted the delights of paradise, which have produced the hellish torments from which I now suffer. She had the disease before me, and she may well be dead by now. Paquette received this present from a very learned Franciscan monk, who was able to trace it back to its primary source. For it came to him from an old countess, who got it from a cavalry captain, who owed it to a marquise, who had it from a page, who caught it from a Jesuit, who during his novitiate received it directly from a shipmate of Christopher Columbus.[15] As for myself, I shall not give it to anyone, for I am dying."

"Oh Pangloss!" exclaimed Candide, "What a strange genealogy! Isn't the devil at the root of it all?"

"Not at all," the great man replied. "It was an indispensable element of the best of worlds, a necessary ingredient. For had Columbus not caught this disease on an American island, this disease which poisons the source of reproduction, which often prevents reproduction entirely, and which is clearly opposed to the great purpose of nature—then we would have neither chocolate nor cochineal.[16] It must also be noted that until now, this malady, like theological conflict, is limited to the European continent. The Turks, Indians, Persians, Chinese, Siamese, and Japanese are not yet acquainted with it. But the principle of sufficient reason will bring it to them as well, in due course of time. Meanwhile, it is making amazing progress among us, especially in those vast armies composed of decent, well-bred scholarship boys,[17] who shape the destiny of nations. You can be sure that when thirty thousand men fight a pitched battle against an equal number of troops, there are about twenty thousand syphilitics on each side."

"Very impressive," said Candide, "but we must get you cured."

"How can I be?" said Pangloss. "I am penniless, my friend, and nowhere on earth can you be bled or get an enema for free."

This last remark made up Candide's mind. He proceeded to throw himself at the feet of his charitable Anabaptist Jacques and painted such a moving picture of his friend's condition that the good man immediately took in Dr. Pangloss and paid for his treatment. In the cure Pangloss lost only one eye and one ear. He could write well and knew arithmetic perfectly. The Anabaptist Jacques made him his bookkeeper. Two months later he was obliged to go to Lisbon on business, and he took his two philosophers with him on the boat. Pangloss explained to him how everything was for the best. Jacques was not convinced.

"Surely," he said, "humankind has corrupted its nature a little, for people were not born wolves, yet they have become wolves. God did not give

---

[15]This account of the transmission of syphilis is a parody of the genealogies recited in the Bible.

[16]Cochineal was a scarlet dye imported from Mexico and Peru. The encounter between the Old World and the New World was an epidemiological disaster. The Europeans transmitted smallpox to the Native Americans, and the natives transmitted syphilis to the Europeans (or so it was believed in Voltaire's time; today there is an unresolved debate about the origins of venereal diseases in Europe).

[17]That is, mercenaries.

them heavy cannon or bayonets, yet they have invented them to destroy each other. I could also refer to bankruptcies, and the system of justice that confiscates a bankrupt man's property just to prevent the creditors from getting it."

"All that is indispensable," replied the one-eyed doctor. "Private misfortunes work for the general good, so the more private misfortunes there are, the more all is well."

While he was theorizing, the sky clouded over, the winds rushed in from the four corners of the globe, and the ship was assailed by a terrible storm just as the port of Lisbon came into view.

CHAPTER 5

Storm, shipwreck, earthquake, and what happened to Dr. Pangloss, Candide, and Jacques the Anabaptist

Half the passengers, weakened and nearly dying from the indescribable agony that the rolling of a ship inflicts on the nerves and humors of a body shaken in different directions, were not even strong enough to recognize how great the danger was. The other half were shrieking and praying. The sails were in shreds, the masts in pieces, the hull split open. Everybody worked who could, but no one cooperated and no one commanded. The Anabaptist was trying to help on the upper deck. A panicked sailor struck him violently and laid him out flat, but his own blow threw him off balance and he fell headfirst over the side. He caught on to part of the broken mast and remained hanging there. The good Jacques got up and ran to his aid, helping him to climb back up; but in the process he was thrown into the sea, right in front of the sailor, who let him drown without even condescending to look at him. Candide rushed over and saw his benefactor appear on the surface for an instant before sinking forever into the deep. He wanted to dive into the sea after him, but the philosopher Pangloss stopped him by demonstrating that the Lisbon harbor was designed expressly for this Anabaptist to drown in. While he was perfecting his logical proof, the ship broke into two and everyone perished except for Pangloss, Candide, and that brutal sailor who had drowned the virtuous Anabaptist. The rogue swam with ease to the shore, while Pangloss and Candide drifted there on a plank.

When they had recovered, they walked toward Lisbon. They still had a little money, with which they hoped to avert hunger after escaping from the storm.

They had scarcely set foot in the city, still mourning the death of their benefactor, when they felt the ground tremble beneath them. The sea boiled up in the port and snapped the ships lying at anchor. Whirlwinds of flame and ashes bellowed through the streets and public squares. Houses crumbled. The roofs collapsed onto their foundations, and then the foundations themselves disintegrated. Thirty thousand inhabitants of every age and sex were crushed in the ruins.

Swearing and whistling, the sailor remarked, "I can get something out of this."

"What can be the sufficient reason for this phenomenon?" asked Pangloss.

"It's the end of the world!" cried Candide.

The sailor jumped into the wreckage without hesitation. He defied death in the search for money, found what he was looking for, seized it, got drunk and, after sobering up a bit, coupled with the first available girl whose favors he could buy, on the ruins of destroyed houses and amid the dead and dying. Pangloss, however, began to tug on his sleeve.

"My friend," he said, "this is not good form. You are ignoring the principles of universal reason; this is not the time or the place."

"By the blood of Christ," said the other, "I am a sailor and was born in Batavia. I have trampled on the cross four times to make my four voyages to Japan—you are knocking on the wrong door here with your universal reason!"[18]

Some falling stones had wounded Candide. He lay flat on the street, covered with debris, calling out to Pangloss, "Alas! Bring me a little wine and oil; I'm dying."

"This earthquake is not a unique phenomenon," Pangloss replied. "The city of Lima in South America experienced the same shocks in South America last year. Same causes, same effects—there must be a vein of sulphur running underground from Lima to Lisbon."

"That's highly probable," said Candide, "but for God's sake, a little oil and wine."

"What do you mean, probable?" retorted the philosopher. "I maintain that the thing is a logical necessity."

Candide lost consciousness, and then Pangloss brought him some water from a nearby fountain.

The next day, as they wandered through the rubble, they found some

---

[18]Having read some accounts of travelers to the Orient, Voltaire believed that Europeans were allowed to trade in Japan only if they first trampled on a crucifix as they entered the country.

food, which partially restored their strength. Then they fell to work with those who were aiding the survivors. Some of the citizens whom they rescued organized a dinner that was as nice as could be expected in such a disaster. The meal was sad, it is true; the guests watered their bread with their tears. Pangloss, however, consoled them with his assurances that things could not be otherwise.

"For," he said, "all this is for the best, for if there is a volcano in Lisbon, it could not be anywhere else. For it is impossible that something be where it is not. For all is well."

A little dark man, a spy of the Inquisition[19] who was seated next to Pangloss, politely spoke up: "Apparently the gentleman does not believe in original sin, for if everything is for the best, then the fall of man and the punishment for sin never took place."

"I very humbly request Your Excellency's pardon," Pangloss responded even more politely. "For the fall of man and the curse that came with it were necessary components of the best of all possible worlds."

"So the gentleman does not believe in free will?" said the spy.

"Excuse me, Your Excellency," said Pangloss, "but freedom can be reconciled with absolute necessity, for it was necessary for us to be endowed with freedom; for, after all, a determined will . . . "

Pangloss was in the middle of his sentence when the spy nodded to the armed attendant who was then pouring him a glass of port wine, otherwise known as Oporto.

CHAPTER 6

How they made a fine auto-da-fé to prevent earthquakes, and how Candide was whipped

When this earthquake, which had destroyed three-quarters of Lisbon, came to an end, the wise men of the land could think of no more effective way of avoiding total ruin than to give the people a fine auto-da-fé.[20] The faculty of the University of Coimbra had concluded that the spectacle of roasting several persons over a slow fire in a ceremonious fashion is an infallible secret for preventing the earth from quaking. They had therefore seized a man from the Basque province who had been convicted

---

[19]Most readers will associate the Inquisition with an earlier time. In fact, it was not abolished until the early nineteenth century.

[20]Literally "act of faith" in Portuguese, an auto-da-fé is the ceremony in which heretics are burned.

of marrying the godmother of his godchild, and two Portuguese men, who when eating a chicken, had removed the bacon seasoning.[21]

After dinner, Dr. Pangloss and his disciple Candide were also arrested, the first for saying what he said, the second for listening with an air of approval. They were led separately to some extremely cool rooms in which no one was ever bothered by the sun.[22] A week later they were both dressed in yellow robes and their heads were adorned with paper caps. Candide's cap and robe were painted with inverted flames and with devils without tails or claws, whereas Pangloss's devils had claws and tails and his flames were right side up.[23] Thus attired, they marched in procession and heard a very touching sermon, followed by charming penitential music. Candide was whipped in cadence with the chant; the man from the Basque province and the two who avoided the bacon were burned; and Pangloss was hanged, though it was not the customary form of execution. The same day the earth shook again with a terrible uproar.

Stunned, stupefied, frantic, bleeding, trembling, Candide thought to himself, "If this is the best of all possible worlds, what are the others like? I can reconcile myself to this beating because I already got one from the Bulgars. But oh, my dear Pangloss! The greatest of all philosophers, was it necessary to see you hanged, without knowing why? Oh, my dear Anabaptist! The best of men, was it necessary for you to drown in the port? Oh! Miss Cunégonde, the pearl of young ladies, was it necessary that your belly be split open?"

Candide left the scene of punishment, barely able to stand, having been lectured, lacerated, absolved, and blessed. But an old woman approached and said, "My son, take courage, follow me."

CHAPTER 7

How an old woman took care of Candide, and how he regained what he had loved

Candide did not take courage, but he followed the old woman into a shack. She gave him a jar of ointment for his wounds and left him food and drink. She showed him to a tidy little bed, with a suit of clothing beside it.

---

[21]The Catholic Church considered a godmother and godfather to be relatives, even if they belonged to different families. Hence, marriage by godparents was condemned as incest. The two Portuguese men are Jewish converts to Catholicism who reveal that they practice their old religion in secret when they remove the unkosher part of the meal.

[22]Prison.

[23]In the ceremony of the Inquisition, the inverted flame showed that the accused had repented; the upright flame meant the accused was impenitent and was going to be burned.

"Eat, drink, sleep," said she, "and may Our Lady of Atocha, My Lord Saint Anthony of Padua, and My Lord Saint James of Compostela take care of you! I will return tomorrow."

Candide, still overwhelmed by all he had seen, all he had suffered, and even more by the old woman's charity, tried to kiss her hand.

"It is not my hand you should kiss," said the old woman. "I will return tomorrow. Use the ointment, eat, and sleep."

Despite his many sufferings, Candide did eat and sleep. The next morning the old woman brought him breakfast, examined his back, and treated it herself with another ointment. Afterwards she brought him lunch, and in the evening, supper. The following day she performed the same ceremonies.

"Who are you?" Candide kept asking. "Who made you so kind? How can I ever repay you?"

The good woman never answered. She came back in the evening, this time without supper.

"Come with me," she said, "and don't say a word."

She took him by the arm and they walked together into the country for a quarter mile. They arrived at an isolated house, surrounded by gardens and ponds. The old woman knocked on a small door. It opened, and she escorted Candide up a concealed staircase, into a gilded chamber, and onto a brocaded couch. Then she closed the door and disappeared. Candide thought he was hallucinating. His life, which had been a nightmare, now seemed like a pleasant dream.

The old woman soon reappeared. With great difficulty she supported a trembling young lady, with a splendid figure, sparkling with jewels, and covered by a veil.

"Remove this veil," said the old woman to Candide.

The young man stepped forward and lifted it with a timid hand. What a moment! What a surprise! He thought he perceived Miss Cunégonde — and he did, for it was she. He grew faint, speech failed him, he fell at her feet. Cunégonde collapsed on the sofa. The old woman plied them with spirits; they came to their senses and spoke to each other. First came broken words, then simultaneous questions and answers, sighs, tears, and moans.[24] The old lady urged them to be more quiet, and left them alone.

"What! It's really you," said Candide. "You are alive! I've found you again in Portugal! Then you were not raped? They didn't slice open your belly as the philosopher Pangloss claimed?"

---

[24]This description of the lovers reuniting is a parody of the sentimental novels of the eighteenth century.

"It did happen," said the lovely Cunégonde, "but one doesn't always die from those two accidents."

"But your father and mother, murdered?"

"Too true," said Cunégonde crying.

"And your brother?"

"Also killed."

"And why are you in Portugal? How did you know I was here? In what mysterious way did you arrange to bring me here?"

"I will tell you everything," replied the lady, "but first you must tell me everything that has happened to you since the innocent kiss you gave me and the violent kicks you received."

Candide obeyed her with deep respect, and though he was still in shock, his voice weak and trembling, and his spine still aching, he related in simple words everything he had suffered since their parting. Cunégonde raised her eyes to heaven. She wept at the death of the good Anabaptist and of Pangloss; after which she spoke in these terms to Candide, who did not miss a word, and who consumed her with his eyes.

CHAPTER 8

Cunégonde's story

"I was sleeping soundly in my bed when heaven chose to send the Bulgars to our fine castle of Thunder-ten-tronckh. They butchered my father and brother and cut my mother to pieces. A large Bulgar, well over six feet tall, seeing that I had fainted at this spectacle, began to rape me; this brought me to and I regained my senses. I shrieked, I struggled, I bit, I scratched, I tried to tear the eyes out of that big Bulgar—not knowing that everything happening then in my father's castle was part of military custom. The brute stabbed me in the belly on the left side, where I still have a scar."

"Alas! I hope to see that," said the simple Candide.

"You will," said Cunégonde, "but let me go on."

"Please go on," said Candide.

She took up the thread of her story: "A Bulgar captain came by. He saw me, all covered in blood, as well as the soldier who was too busy to salute him. Enraged by the brute's lack of respect for his rank, the captain killed him while he was still on top of my body. Then he had my wound dressed and took me to his quarters as a prisoner of war. I laundered the few shirts he had, I did his cooking. I have to admit, he found me attractive, and I won't deny that he was a handsome man, with soft, white skin. But he had no intellect, no philosophy; it was clear that he had not been raised by Dr. Pangloss. Three months later, he had lost all his money and grown sick of me, so he sold me to Don Issachar, a Jew who traded in Holland and Portugal and who had a passionate taste for women. This Jew took a great liking to my person, but he never conquered it. I resisted him better than I did the Bulgar soldier. A lady of honor may be raped once, but it strengthens her virtue for the future. In order to tame me, the Jew brought me to this country house. I always used to think there was nothing on earth so beautiful as the castle of Thunder-ten-tronckh. I have that illusion no longer.

"The Grand Inquisitor noticed me one day at mass. He ogled me and sent me a message that he had to speak to me about secret affairs. I was escorted to his palace, where I informed him of my high birth. He pointed out how much it was beneath my rank to belong to an Israelite. His agents suggested to Don Issachar to cede me to His Lordship. But Don Issachar, who is the court banker and a man of prestige, flatly refused. The Inquisitor threatened him with an auto-da-fé. Finally, my Jew, intimidated, made a deal whereby the house and I belong to them jointly: the Jew would get Mondays, Wednesdays, and the Sabbath, and the Inquisitor all other days of the week. The contract has lasted six months, though not without quarrels, because they have never been able to decide if the night between Saturday and Sunday belongs to the old Sabbath or the new. As for me, I've resisted them both so far, and I think that's why their love for me has been so strong.

"Finally, to ward off the scourge of earthquakes and to intimidate Issachar, the Inquisitor decided to celebrate an auto-da-fé. He honored me with an invitation. I had a very good seat and they served refreshments to the ladies between the mass and the execution. I was truly gripped by horror when I saw them burn the two Jews and that upright fellow from the Basque country who had married his godchild's godmother. But imagine my surprise, my terror, my agitation, when I saw, in a yellow robe and underneath a paper cap, a form resembling Pangloss! I rubbed my eyes, I peered closely, I saw him hanged, I fainted. I had scarcely recovered my senses when I saw you, stripped down naked. This was the height of my horror, consternation, pain, and despair. I will tell you, in truth, that your skin is even whiter, and more delightfully tinted with pink, than that of my Bulgar captain. This sight redoubled all the emotions that were crushing me, devouring me. I cried out, I tried to say, 'Stop, barbarians!' but my voice failed and my cries would have been futile. After you had been thoroughly whipped, I began to think: 'How can it be that the gentle Candide and the wise Pangloss have come to Lisbon, one to receive a hundred lashes, the other to be hanged by order of the Inquisitor whose mistress I am? Pangloss deceived me cruelly when he taught me that everything is for the best in this world.'

"Frantic and exhausted, half out of my mind and half on the verge of expiring from weakness, my head was filled with images of my murdered father, mother, and brother; of the insolence of my vile Bulgar soldier and the slashing he inflicted on me; of my servitude as a cook to my Bulgar captain; of my vile Don Issacher and my abominable Inquisitor; of the hanging of Dr. Pangloss and the solemn hymn of penitence sung while they whipped you; and above all, of the kiss I once gave you behind a partition, the day I saw you for the last time. I praised God for bringing you back to me after so many ordeals. I asked my old servant to take care of you and to bring you here as soon as she could. She has done the job well. I have tasted the indescribable pleasure of seeing you, hearing you, speaking to you again. But you must be burning with hunger. My desire is strong. Let us begin with supper."

So they sat down to table together, and after supper they installed themselves on that lovely couch that was already mentioned. There they were, when Señor Don Issachar, one of the masters of the house, arrived. It was the Sabbath day. He had come to enjoy his rights and to profess his tender love.

CHAPTER 9

What happened to Cunégonde, Candide, the Grand Inquisitor, and a Jew

This Issachar was the most hot-tempered Hebrew seen in Israel since the Babylonian captivity.

"What!" he said. "You Christian bitch, you are not satisfied with the Inquisitor? I have to share you with this scoundrel too?"

With these words he unsheathed a long dagger that he always carried with him, and supposing his adversary to be defenseless, flung himself at Candide. But our good Westphalian had gotten a fine sword from the old woman along with the suit of clothes. Though his character was gentle, he drew his sword and laid the Israelite out cold and stiff on the floor, at the feet of the beautiful Cunégonde.

"Holy Virgin!" she cried. "What are we going to do now? A man killed in my house! If the police come, we're finished."

"If Pangloss had not been hanged," said Candide, "he would offer us good advice in this emergency, for he was a great philosopher. In his absence, let's consult the old woman."

She was a prudent woman and was about to give her opinion when another little door opened. It was one o'clock in the morning, the beginning of Sunday. This day belonged to the Inquisitor. He came in and saw the whipped Candide with a sword in his hand, a dead man on the floor, Cunégonde in panic, and the old woman advising them.

This is what went on at that instant in Candide's mind, and how he theorized: "If this holy man calls for help, he will infallibly have me burned, and perhaps Cunégonde too; he has caused me to be whipped brutally; he is my rival; I have killed once already; there is no time to hesitate."

This reflection was swift and clear. Without giving the Inquisitor time to recover from his surprise, he ran his sword through his body, and cast him beside the Jew.

"You've done it again," said Cunégonde. "We're beyond salvation now; we're excommunicated, our last hour has come. How have you managed, you who are so gentle, to kill a Jew and a prelate in two minutes?"

"My fair lady," answered Candide, "when a man is in love, inflamed by jealousy, and whipped by the Inquisition, he is no longer himself."

The old woman spoke up at that moment: "There are three Andalusian horses in the stable, with saddles and bridles. Let the brave Candide prepare them. My Lady has some diamonds and gold coins. Let us mount quickly—though I can sit on only one buttock—and ride to Cadiz. The weather is ideal, and it is a great pleasure to travel in the cool of the night."

Candide immediately saddled the three horses. The three of them covered thirty miles at one stretch. While they were getting away, the officers of the Holy Brotherhood[25] arrived at the house. They buried the Inquisitor in a fine church, and threw Issachar in the public dump.

Candide, Cunégonde, and the old woman were already at an inn in the little town of Avacena in the middle of the Sierra-Morena mountains, and they spoke as follows.

CHAPTER 10

How Candide, Cunégonde, and the old woman arrived at Cadiz in distress, and how they set sail

"Who could have stolen my gold and my diamonds?" exclaimed Cunégonde, weeping. "What are we going to live on now? What are we going to do? Where can I find Inquisitors and Jews who will give me more?"

[25]A religious order with police powers in Spain.

"Alas," said the old woman, "I strongly suspect a venerable Franciscan who slept at the same inn with us yesterday at Badajoz. God forgive me if my judgment is rash, but he came into our chamber twice, and he left the inn long before we did."

"Alas," said Candide, "the wise Pangloss often proved to me that the goods of the earth are common to all men, that everyone has an equal right to them. By this logic, the Franciscan should have left us enough to finish our journey. Didn't he leave you anything at all, my lovely Cunégonde?"

"Not a cent," said she.

"What is our plan?" Candide asked.

"We must sell one of the horses," said the old woman. "I will ride on the horse's rump behind my lady—though I can sit on only one buttock—and we will travel to Cadiz."

There was a Bendectine prior staying in the same inn. He bought the horse at a low price. Candide, Cunégonde, and the old woman passed through Lucena, Chillas, and Lebrixa, and finally reached Cadiz. A fleet was being fitted out there, and troops were being assembled to teach a lesson to the Jesuit fathers in Paraguay. The Jesuits had been accused of inciting one of the tribes near the town of Sacramento to revolt against the kings of Spain and Portugal.[26] Candide, having served in the Bulgar army, performed a Bulgar drill in front of the general of the little army with such grace, speed, skill, pride, and agility that he was put in charge of a company of infantry. He was a captain now. He embarked with Miss Cunégonde, the old woman, two valets, and the two Andalusian horses that had belonged to the Grand Inquisitor of Portugal.

Throughout the crossing, they theorized at length about the philosophy of poor Pangloss.

"We are heading for a different world," said Candide. "I am sure that over there all is well, because I have to admit that where we come from, there are grounds for complaining about how things are, both physically and morally."

"I love you with all my heart," Cunégonde told him, "but my soul is still terrified by what I have seen and endured."

"All will be well," Candide replied. "The sea of this New World is superior to the sea of our Europe; it is calmer, with steadier winds. I am certain the New World is the best of all possible universes."

---

[26]Sacramento was a colony in Paraguay contested by the Spanish and Portuguese. Some of the missionaries were accused of inciting a revolt by the natives against the European rulers. In 1755–56, Spain sent troops to put down the uprising. This is the expedition for which Candide is recruited.

"May God grant that it be so," said Cunégonde. But my universe has been so terribly unhappy that my heart is nearly closed to the possibility of hope."

"The two of you are complaining," the old woman said to them. "Alas! You have never seen misfortunes like mine."

Cunégonde almost burst out laughing. She found it amusing that the good woman claimed to be more unhappy than herself.

"Alas!" she said. "My dear woman, unless you have been raped by two Bulgars, been stabbed in the belly twice, seen two of your castles demolished, witnessed the murder of two mothers and fathers, and watched two of your lovers being whipped in an auto-da-fé, I don't see how you can outdo me. Besides, I was born to be a baroness, with seventy-two generations of nobility, and I was forced to be a cook."

"Madame," replied the old woman, "you know nothing of my birth, and if I showed you my behind, you would speak differently and suspend your judgment."

These remarks aroused intense curiosity in the minds of Cunégonde and Candide. The old woman spoke to them in these terms.

CHAPTER 11

The old woman's story

"My eyes were not always crusty and bloodshot, my nose did not always touch my chin, and I was not always a servant. I am the daughter of Pope Urban X and the Princess of Palestrina.[27] I lived until the age of fourteen in a palace so luxurious that all the castles of your German barons would not have served as stables. Any one of my dresses was worth more than all the treasures of Westphalia. I was growing in beauty, elegance, and accomplishment in the midst of pleasures, honors, and the highest hopes. I was beginning to inspire love. My bosom was forming, and what a bosom! White, firm, sculptured like the ancient statue of Venus. And what eyes! What lashes! What black brows! What flames blazed in my irises and sparkled brighter than the stars, as the local poets used to tell me. The women who dressed and undressed me fell into ecstasies when

---

[27]Among Voltaire's manuscripts is a remark on this passage that he may have intended to add as a footnote to future editions of *Candide:* "Observe the author's extreme discretion! Until now there has never been any pope named Urban X. He stops short of attributing a bastard to a known pope. Oh, what circumspection! Oh, what delicacy of conscience!"

they beheld me from the front and from the rear, and any man would have desired to be in their place.

"I was betrothed to the ruling prince of Massa-Carrara. What a prince! As attractive as I, filled with sweetness and delight, with a brilliant wit and burning passion. I loved him as one always loves for the first time, with adoration and frenzy. The wedding was at hand. The pomp and splendor were unprecedented. It was an endless series of feasts, equestrian tournaments, comic operas, and all Italy honored me with sonnets of which not a single one was any good.

"I was on the verge of bliss, when an old marquise who had been my prince's mistress invited him for a cup of cocoa. He died in less than two hours, in horrible convulsions. But that was only a trifle. My mother, stricken with grief, though less than I, wished to escape from this tragic scene for a while. She had a very fine estate near Gaeta. Our transport was a papal galley ship, gilded like the altar of St. Peter's in Rome. Suddenly a pirate ship from Salé swept down and boarded us.[28] Our soldiers defended themselves like true soldiers of the Pope: they all kneeled down, threw aside their arms, and begged the pirates for absolution *in articulo mortis.*[29]

"The pirates immediately stripped them naked as monkeys, along with my mother, our ladies-in-waiting, and myself. The speed with which those gentlemen can undress people is amazing. But what surprised me even more was that they inserted their fingers in all of us, in a place where we women usually admit only the nozzle of an enema. This ceremony seemed quite bizarre to me; but that is how one sees everything foreign when one has never been abroad. I soon learned that they wished to see if we had diamonds hidden there. It is an age-old custom among the civilized people who patrol the seas. I also learned that the pious Knights of Malta always observe this ceremony when they capture Turkish men and women. It's a rule of international law that has never been broken.

"I will not tell you how hard it is for a young princess to be dragged off to Morocco as a slave with her mother. You can imagine everything we had to endure in the pirate ship. My mother was still beautiful; our ladies-in-waiting and even our ordinary servants had more charm than could be found in all of Africa. As for me, I was ravishing, I was beauty and grace made flesh, and I was a virgin. But not for long. The flower I had reserved for the handsome prince of Massa-Carrara was plucked by the pirate captain. He was an abominable Negro who thought he was

---

[28]Salé, on the coast of Morocco, was a center of piracy in the eighteenth century.
[29]At the point of death.

bestowing great favors on me. The Princess of Palestrina and I certainly had to be very strong to withstand everything we went through up to our arrival in Morocco. But we can skip the details; these things are so common that they are not worth describing.

"Morocco was swimming in blood when we arrived. Fifty sons of the Emperor Muley Ismael each had his own faction, which produced fifty civil wars of blacks against blacks, blacks against browns, browns against browns, mulattoes against mulattoes. There was constant slaughter throughout the empire.[30]

"Scarcely had we landed when some blacks of a faction hostile to my pirate came on the scene to take away the booty. We were, after the diamonds and gold, his most precious possessions. The fight that took place before my eyes was worse than anything you ever see in your European climates. The peoples of the North do not have hot blood. Their lust for women is not as strong as it is in Africa. It is as if Europeans have milk in their veins, while vitriol and fire flow through the veins of the inhabitants of Mount Atlas and the countries nearby. They fought to possess us with the fury of the lions, tigers, and vipers of their land. A Moor snatched my mother by the right arm, my captain's lieutenant held her by the left. Another Moorish soldier took her by one leg, one of our pirates clung to the other. Nearly all our women were quickly pulled in this way by four soldiers. My captain shielded me behind him. Brandishing his scimitar, he killed everyone who stood up to his rage. At last I saw all our women, and then my mother, ripped and sliced and massacred by the monsters who were fighting over them. The other hostages, the pirates who had captured them, the soldiers, sailors, blacks, browns, whites, mulattoes, and finally my captain—all were killed, and I myself lay dying on a heap of corpses. As everyone knows, scenes like this were occurring for more than seven hundred and fifty miles around, without anyone failing to observe the five daily prayers prescribed by Mohammed.

"I freed myself with great difficulty from that tangled mob of bleeding cadavers and I crawled under a large orange tree on the bank of a nearby stream. There I collapsed from fear, exhaustion, horror, despair, and hunger. Soon my weary mind surrendered to an oblivion that was more of a frightful blackout than a pleasant repose. I was in that state of weakness and insensibility, between life and death, when I felt the pressure of

[30]This description is loosely historical. The Sultan of Morocco, Muley Ismael, reigned for fifty years; his death in 1727 plunged the country into civil war.

something wriggling on my body. I opened my eyes and saw a white man with a handsome face who was moaning and whispering, *'O che sciagura d'essere senza coglioni!'*[31]

CHAPTER 12

Continuation of the old woman's story

"Astonished and delighted to hear my native tongue, and equally surprised by the words this man was uttering, I replied that there were worse misfortunes than the one he was complaining of. I gave him a brief account of my own horrors, and fainted again. He carried me to a nearby house, put me to bed, fed me, waited on me, comforted me, flattered me, and told me he had never seen anything as beautiful as I, and that he had never so much regretted the loss of what no one could ever give back to him.

" 'I was born in Naples,' he told me, 'where they castrate two or three thousand children every year. Some die as a result, others acquire the ability to sing more beautifully than women, still others go on to rule states. In my case, the operation was a great success, and I became a musician in the chapel of the Princess of Palestrina.'

" 'Of my mother!' I cried out.

" 'Of your mother?' he exclaimed, while bursting into tears. 'Why— are you that little princess I brought up to the age of six, and who even then promised to be as gorgeous as you are now?'

" 'Yes, I am. My mother is four hundred paces away, cut into four pieces, under a pile of corpses . . . '

"I told him everything that happened to me, and he in turn told me of his adventures. He had been sent to the King of Morocco by a Christian power to conclude a treaty: the King was supposed to receive gunpowder, cannons, and ships and use these to exterminate the commerce of other Christian powers.[32]

" 'My mission is accomplished,' said the worthy eunuch. 'I am setting sail to Ceuta, and I shall bring you back to Italy. But *che sciagura d'essere senza coglioni!'*

---

[31]"Oh, what an affliction to be without balls!"

[32]For the European countries of the Mediterranean, trade with North Africa was a principal source of wealth. The eunuch was sent to Morocco to conclude a treaty that would confer trading privileges on the country he represented.

"I thanked him with tears of gratitude and pity; and instead of bringing me to Italy, he transported me to Algiers and sold me to the Dey of that province. Hardly had the sale taken place, when the plague, which was sweeping over Africa, Asia, and Europe, broke out violently in Algiers.[33] You have seen earthquakes, but tell me, young lady, have you ever had the plague?"

"Never," replied the Baron's daughter.

"If you had been afflicted with it," the old woman went on, "you would admit that it is much worse than an earthquake. It is very widespread in Africa, and I was struck by it. Imagine the situation of a pope's daughter, only fifteen years old, who in the space of three months had undergone poverty and slavery, had been raped almost every day, had seen her mother cut in four pieces, had endured hunger and war, and now faced death from the plague in Algiers. As it turned out, I survived, but my eunuch, the Dey, and nearly the whole harem of Algiers, perished.

"When the first ravages of this ghastly plague were over, the Dey's slaves were sold off. A merchant purchased me and brought me to Tunis. He sold me to another merchant, who sold me once more in Tripoli. From Tripoli I was resold to Alexandria, from Alexandria to Smyrna, from Smyrna to Constantinople. In the end I belonged to an Aga[34] of the Janissaries, who was shortly sent off to defend Azov against the attacking Russians.[35]

"The Aga, a very gallant man, took his whole harem with him, and lodged us in a little fort on the shore of the Sea of Azov, guarded by two black eunuchs and twenty soldiers. Our side killed a prodigious number of Russians, but they repaid us with interest. The settlement at Azov was put to fire and sword, and neither women nor children were spared. The last place left was our little fort. The enemy tried to starve us out. The twenty Janissaries had sworn never to surrender. When they became famished, they were obliged to eat our two eunuchs, for fear of breaking their oath. A few days later they resolved to eat the women.

"We had with us a very pious and compassionate imam,[36] who preached a fine sermon, persuading them not to kill us altogether. 'Just cut off one buttock from each of these ladies,' he said, 'and you will dine well. If you need more, you can have the same fare in a few days. You will

---

[33]The dreadful bubonic plague, the most lethal disease in human history, continued to ravage southern France and the Levant well into the eighteenth century.

[34]A general of the Janissaries or elite mercenary units of the Turkish army.

[35]In 1695–97, to gain access to the Black Sea, the Russian Tsar, Peter the Great, besieged Azov, then a part of the Turkish Empire.

[36]A Muslim priest.

please heaven with such a charitable deed, and you will be saved from this calamity.'

"He was very eloquent and persuaded them. They performed the horrible operation on us. The imam rubbed us with the same balm that they put on children who have just been circumcised. We were all nearly dead.

"Scarcely had the Janissaries finished the meal we had furnished them, when more Russians arrived in flat-bottomed boats; not a single Janissary escaped alive. The Russians paid no attention to our condition. But there are French doctors everywhere, and one of them, who was very clever, took care of us. He cured us, and I will remember to the end of my life that when my wounds were healed, he made advances to me. Besides that, he told us all to take comfort. He assured us that such things usually happened in sieges and that it was one of the rules of war.

"As soon as my companions and I could walk, we were sent off to Moscow. I fell to the lot of a Boyar, who made me his gardener and gave me twenty lashes per day. But when this noble was broken on the wheel two years later, along with thirty or so other Boyars, over a little intrigue at the royal court, I took advantage of the incident.[37] I fled. I traversed the whole of Russia. For a long time I was a barmaid in Riga, then in Rostock, Wismar, Leipzig, Cassel, Utrecht, Leyden, the Hague, and Rotterdam. I have grown old in misery and infamy, with only half a behind, and never forgetting that I was the daughter of a Pope.

"I considered suicide a hundred times, but I still loved life. That ridiculous preference is perhaps one of our most tragic instincts. For what could be more stupid than this: to seek to carry forever a weight that we always feel like casting to the ground? To view our existence with horror, and to cling tightly to our existence? To caress the snake that devours us, until it has consumed our heart?

"In the countries that fate made me traverse, and in the inns where I worked, I have seen vast numbers of people who detested their own lives; but I have seen only twelve who voluntarily brought an end to their suffering — three Negroes, four Englishmen, four Genevans, and a German professor named Robek.[38] I ended up becoming a servant to the Jew, Don Issachar. He assigned me to you, my lovely Lady. I have attached myself to your destiny, and I have been more concerned with your fortune than my own. I would never have spoken about my sufferings had you not provoked me a bit, and were it not the custom on ships to pass

---

[37]The Boyars were a class of Russian nobles. Two years after the siege of Azov, a conspiracy against Peter the Great, known as the "revolt of the streltsy," did in fact take place.

[38]Johann Robek, or Robeck (1672–1739), who wrote a book justifying suicide, drowned himself. The morality of suicide was often debated during the Enlightenment.

the time with stories. In short, My Lady, I have some experience, I know the world. I propose that you amuse yourselves by asking each passenger to tell you his story, and if you find a single one who has not frequently cursed his own life, who has not often told himself that he was the unhappiest of men, then throw me into the sea headfirst."

CHAPTER 13

How Candide was forced to part from the lovely Cunégonde and the old woman

After hearing the old woman's story, the lovely Cunégonde showed her all the courtesy due to a person of her rank and merit. She accepted the old woman's proposal too, and got all the passengers, one by one, to recount their life stories. She and Candide had to admit that the old woman was right.

"It's too bad," said Candide, "that the wise Pangloss was hanged, contrary to custom, in an auto-da-fé. He would say admirable things about the physical and moral evil that cover land and sea, and I would now be independent enough to make a few respectful objections."

As each passenger was telling his story, the vessel sailed on. They landed at Buenos Aires. Cunégonde, Captain Candide, and the old woman proceeded to the home of Governor Don Fernando d'Ibaraa y Figueora y Mascarenes y Lampourdos y Souza. This lord had the pride appropriate to a man with so many names. He addressed people with the most noble disdain, tilting his nose so high in the air, raising his voice so mercilessly, adopting so imperious a tone, affecting so haughty a bearing, that everyone who met him wanted to beat him up. He loved women with a frenzy, and Cunégonde seemed to him the most beautiful creature he had ever seen. The first thing he did was to ask if she were the Captain's wife. His manner of asking the question alarmed Candide. He did not dare say she was his wife, because in fact she was not. He did not dare say she was his sister, because she was not that either; and even though this diplomatic lie was once very fashionable among the ancients[39] and can still be useful to the moderns, his soul was too pure to forsake the truth.

"Miss Cunégonde," he said, "will soon honor me by becoming my wife, and we humbly beseech Your Excellency to perform the ceremony."

Don Fernando d'Ibaraa y Figueora y Mascarenes y Lampourdos y

---

[39] An allusion to Abraham's ruse in Genesis, 20:11–16.

Souza stroked his mustache, and with a spiteful smile ordered Captain Candide to go off and inspect his troops. Candide obeyed, while the Governor remained with Miss Cunégonde. He declared his passion and vowed he would marry her the next day, in the presence of the Catholic Church or in any other manner that would please her loveliness. Cunégonde requested fifteen minutes to gather her thoughts, to consult the old woman, and to make a decision.

The old woman said to Cunégonde, "My Lady, you have seventy-two generations of nobility, and not a penny. You now have a chance to be the wife of a man who is the greatest lord in South America and who has a very handsome mustache. Is this a time for you to pretend to be absolutely faithful? You were raped by the Bulgars. A Jew and an Inquisitor enjoyed your favors.[40] Suffering bestows privileges. If I were in your place, I assure you, I would have no qualms about marrying the Governor and securing the welfare of Captain Candide."

While the old woman was speaking with all the prudence that comes from age and experience, a little ship was seen entering the port carrying a Spanish magistrate and police officers. This is what happened.

The old woman had been quite right earlier when she suspected that it was a long-sleeved Franciscan who had stolen Cunégonde's gold and jewels in the town of Badajoz when she and Candide were in flight. The monk had tried to sell some of the gems to a jeweler, but the merchant recognized them as belonging to the Grand Inquisitor. The Franciscan, prior to his hanging, confessed that he had stolen them. He described the persons he had robbed and the route they were taking. It was already known that Cunégonde and Candide had fled. They were traced to Cadiz. A ship was sent to pursue them without delay. This vessel was now in the port of Buenos Aires. A rumor spread that a magistrate was coming ashore to prosecute the murderers of the Grand Inquisitor. The prudent old woman instantly recognized what had to be done.

"You cannot escape," she told Cunégonde, "but you have nothing to fear. You are not the one who killed the Inquisitor, and besides, the Governor loves you and will not tolerate anyone who mistreats you. Stay here."

She then sped off to Candide. "Run away," she said, "or you will be burned within an hour."

There was not a moment to lose—but how to part from Cunégonde, and where to hide?

---

[40]This contradicts Cunégonde's claim in Chapter 8 that she "resisted" the advances of the two men.

CHAPTER 14

How Candide and Cacambo were received by the Jesuits in Paraguay

Candide had brought with him from Cadiz a valet of the kind often found on the coasts of Spain and in the colonies. He was one quarter Spanish, the child of a half-breed father in Tucuman.[41] He had been a choir boy, a sacristan, a sailor, a monk, a salesman, a soldier, and a lackey. His name was Cacambo, and he was very attached to his master because his master was a very good man. He saddled the two Andalusian horses as fast as possible.

"Let's go, Master, let's follow the old woman's advice. Let's get out of here and run for it without looking back."

Candide shed tears. "Oh, my darling Cunégonde! Why must I abandon you now, when the Governor is about to marry us? Cunégonde, so far from home, what will become of you?"

"She'll manage on her own," said Cacambo. "Women always find ways to keep themselves afloat; God sees to it; let's move."

"Where are you taking me? Where are we going? What will we do without Cunégonde?" asked Candide.

"By St. James of Compostela," said Cacambo, "you were going to make war against the Jesuits; let's go make war *for* them! I know the roads, I'll take you to their kingdom. They'll be pleased to have a captain who can move like a Bulgar. You'll become fabulously wealthy. If a man doesn't get his due in one world, he can always get it in another. It's a great pleasure to see and do new things."

"So you've been in Paraguay before?" asked Candide.

"I certainly have," said Cacambo. "I was a cook at the College of the Assumption, and I know the government of the *Padres*[42] as well as I know the streets of Cadiz. Their government is marvellous. The kingdom is already more than seven hundred and fifty miles across. It is divided into thirty provinces. The *Padres* have everything, the people nothing. It's a masterpiece of reason and justice. Personally, I can't think of anything as heavenly as the *Padres*. Over here they make war against the kings of Spain and Portugal, and in Europe they hear the confessions of the same kings. Here they kill Spaniards, and in Madrid they send them to heaven. I love it. Let's get going. You're going to be the happiest of men. What

---

[41]In other words, his mother was a South American Indian, his father was half Indian, half European. Tucuman is a province of Argentina.
[42]The Jesuit Fathers.

pleasure the *Padres* will feel when they learn that a Captain is coming who knows how to move like a Bulgar!"

As soon as they approached the first border post, Cacambo told the advance guards that a captain wished to speak to the Commander. Word was sent back to the rear guards, and a Paraguayan officer ran to inform the Commander. Candide and Cacambo were first disarmed, and their Andalusian horses were confiscated. The two strangers were escorted through two files of soldiers, at the end of which was the Commander, with a three-cornered hat on his head, a tucked-up gown, a sword at his side, and a short pike in his hand. He made a sign, and immediately twenty-four soldiers surrounded the two newcomers. A sergeant told them that they would have to wait, that the Commander could not speak to them and that the Reverend Provincial Father did not allow any Spaniard to parley except in his presence, or to remain in the country for more than three hours.

"And where is the Reverend Provincial Father?" asked Cacambo.

"He is inspecting the troops, after having said Mass," answered the sergeant, "and you will not be allowed to kiss his spurs until three hours from now."

"But," Cacambo said, "the Captain and I are dying of hunger, and he's not Spanish at all, he's German. Couldn't we have something for breakfast while we wait for His Reverence?"

The sergeant promptly went to report this speech to the Commander.

"God be praised!" said this Lord. "Since he is a German, I can speak to him. Bring him to my arbor."

Candide was immediately led into a shady retreat adorned with a pretty colonnade in green and golden marble and with trellises containing parrots, hummingbirds of different kinds, guinea fowl, and every other sort of rare bird. An excellent meal was prepared in gold vessels, and while the Paraguayans were eating corn out of wooden bowls in the open fields, under the blazing sun, the Commander entered the arbor.

He was a very handsome young man, with a round face, fair skin, red cheeks, arched eyebrows, bright eyes, pink ears, and vermillion lips; he had a proud bearing, but it was not the pride of a Spaniard or a Jesuit. The confiscated weapons were restored to Candide and Cacambo, as were the two Andalusian horses. Cacambo fed them oats beside the arbor, keeping a close eye on them, for fear of a new assault.

Candide first kissed the hem of the Commander's robe, then they sat down to eat.

"So, you are German," said the Jesuit in that language.

"Yes, Reverend Father," said Candide.

As they uttered these words, each looked at the other with extreme surprise, and with barely controlled emotion.

"And what part of Germany are you from?" asked the Jesuit.

"From the rotten Province of Westphalia," said Candide. "I was born in the castle of Thunder-ten-tronckh."

"Oh heaven! Is it possible!" exclaimed the Commander.

"What a miracle!" cried Candide.

"Can it be you?" said the Commander.

"This is not possible," said Candide.

They both fell over backwards; they embraced; they shed streams of tears.

"What! Is it really you, my Reverend Father? You, the brother of the lovely Cunégonde! You, who were killed by the Bulgars! You, the son of My Lord the Baron! You, a Jesuit in Paraguay! I have to admit, the world is a very strange place. Oh Pangloss! Pangloss! How happy you would be if you had not been hanged!"

The Commander dismissed the Negro slaves and the Paraguayans who were serving drinks in goblets of rock crystal. He thanked God and St. Ignatius a thousand times. He clasped Candide in his arms; their faces were bathed in tears.

"You're going to be even more surprised, more moved, more beside yourself," said Candide, "when I tell you that your sister, Miss Cunégonde, whom you thought was disemboweled, is in good health."

"Where?"

"In this area, with the Governor of Buenos Aires. I was supposed to help him fight you."

Every word they spoke during their long conversation revealed a new wonder. Their souls leapt from their tongues, drew in meaning through their ears, and sparkled brilliantly in their eyes. As they were Germans, they drank for a long time while they waited for the Reverend Provincial Father; and the Commander spoke to Candide as follows.

CHAPTER 15

How Candide killed the brother of his beloved Cunégonde

"The horrible day when I saw my mother and father killed, and my sister raped, will remain in my memory forever. When the Bulgars withdrew, my adorable sister was nowhere to be found. A cart was loaded with my mother, my father, myself, two serving girls, and three little boys whose throats had been slit. We were to be buried in a Jesuit chapel five miles from the castle of my ancestors. A Jesuit sprinkled holy water on us; it was horribly salty, and a few drops of it got into my eyes. The priest noticed a slight movement of my eyelid. He placed his hand on my heart and felt it beating. I was treated, and three weeks later, I was in good shape again.

"You know, my dear Candide, I was a very pretty boy; I became even more so; and the Reverend Father Croust,[43] superior of the abbey, conceived a very tender friendship for me. He dressed me in the gown of a novice, and soon after that I was sent to Rome. The Father General needed a fresh set of young German Jesuit recruits. The rulers of Paraguay take in as few Spanish Jesuits as they can. They prefer foreigners because they think they can control them better. The Reverend Father General judged me fit to labor in this vineyard. We set out, a Pole, a Tyrolean, and I. Upon arrival, I was honored with the position of subdeacon and lieutenant. Today I am a colonel and a priest. We will give an energetic reception to the King of Spain's troops. I guarantee you they will be excommunicated and defeated. Providence has sent you here to help us. But is it true that my beloved sister Cunégonde is in the region, with the Governor of Buenos Aires?"

Candide assured him by swearing that nothing was more true. They began to shed tears all over again.

The Baron embraced Candide repeatedly, calling him his brother, his savior.

"Ah! My dear Candide," he said, "perhaps we can enter the city as conquerors and liberate my sister Cunégonde."

"I certainly hope so," said Candide, "because I was planning to marry her, and still am."

"You insolent swine!" replied the Baron. "You would have the impudence to marry my sister, who has seventy-two generations of nobility! I find it highly offensive that you dare to mention such an impossible plan to me."

Candide, petrified by this speech, answered him, "My Reverend Father, all the generations in the world make no difference. I rescued your sister from the arms of a Jew and an Inquisitor. She owes me a great deal, she wants to marry me. Dr. Pangloss always taught me that men are equal, and I am certainly going to marry her."

"We shall see about that, you scoundrel," said the Jesuit Baron Thunder-ten-tronckh, and in that instant he dealt him a great blow across

---

[43]The name of a German Jesuit with whom Voltaire quarreled in the 1750s.

the face with the flat side of his sword. Candide rapidly drew his own and thrust it into the Jesuit Baron's stomach, right up to the hilt. But when he drew out the steaming weapon, he began to weep.

"Alas, my God!" he said. "I've killed my old master, my friend, my brother-in-law. I'm the kindest man in the world, and here I've already killed three men—and two of them were priests."

Cacambo, who was standing guard at the gate to the arbor, ran in.

"There's nothing left to do but to make them pay dearly for our lives," his master told him. "They'll surely come into the arbor now; we must die with sword in hand."

Cacambo, who had seen the likes of this many times before, did not lose his head. He took the Jesuit robe that the Baron was wearing, put it on Candide, gave him the dead man's cornered hat, and had him mount his horse. All this was done in the twinkling of an eye.

"Let's gallop, Master. Everyone will take you for a Jesuit on a field mission, and we'll cross the border before they can come after us."

He was already charging ahead as he spoke, and then he cried out in Spanish, "Make way, make way for the Reverend Father Colonel!"

CHAPTER 16

What happened to the two travelers with two girls, two monkeys, and the savages called Oreillons

Candide and his valet had crossed the frontier, and still no one back at camp knew about the German Jesuit's death. The astute Cacambo had taken care to fill his saddlebag with bread, chocolate, ham, fruit, and some bottles of wine. With their Andalusian horses they plunged into an unknown land where they found no roads. Finally, a beautiful meadow, interlaced with streams, appeared before them. Our two travelers freed their horses to graze. Cacambo advised his master to eat, and he began to set the example.

"How do you expect me to eat ham," said Candide, "when I just killed the son of My Lord the Baron and find myself condemned never to see the lovely Cunégonde again? What's the use of prolonging my miserable days, if I have to endure them far away from her, in remorse and despair? And what will the *Journal de Trévoux* say?"[44]

---

[44]The *Journal de Trévoux* was a Jesuit periodical that often published articles critical of the philosophers of the Enlightenment.

While speaking in this way, he did not fail to eat. The sun began to set. The two wanderers heard some faint cries that seemed to proceed from women. They could not tell if these were cries of pain or joy, but they jumped to their feet with that anxiety and alarm that everything arouses in an unknown country.

The sounds came from two girls, completely nude, who were running spryly along the edge of the meadow, while two monkeys pursued them, snapping at their buttocks. Candide was moved by pity. The Bulgars had taught him how to shoot, and he was able to knock a nut off a bush without stirring the leaves. He raised his double-barreled musket from Spain, fired, and killed the two monkeys.

"God be praised, my dear Cacambo. I've rescued these two poor creatures from a great danger. If I committed a sin in killing an Inquisitor and a Jesuit, I've now redeemed myself by saving the lives of two girls. Perhaps these two young ladies are of noble birth, and my deed will bring us great rewards in this land."

He was going to say more, but his tongue became paralyzed when he saw the girls tenderly embrace the two monkeys, burst into tears over their bodies, and fill the air with cries of intense grief.

"I didn't expect them to be so forgiving," he said, after a long pause, to Cacambo, who replied: "That was a brilliant thing to do, Sir! You just killed the young ladies' lovers."

"Their lovers! Is that possible? You must be joking. What evidence do you have?"

"My dear Master," responded Cacambo, "you're always surprised by everything. Why do you find it so bizarre that in some countries monkeys obtain the favors of the ladies? They are a quarter human, just as I am a quarter Spanish."

"Alas!" said Candide. "I do recall hearing Dr. Pangloss say that such things used to happen, that these mixtures engendered pans, fauns, and satyrs, and that many of the heroes of ancient times saw them. But I thought that was all a fable."

"Now you should be convinced that it's the truth," said Cacambo, "and you can see how this truth is still practiced by people who have not been educated. But I'm afraid these ladies are going to make big trouble for us."

These solid reflections persuaded Candide to leave the meadow and plunge into a forest. He dined there with Cacambo, and the two of them, after cursing the Inquisitor of Portugal, the Governor of Buenos Aires, and the Baron, fell asleep on the moss. When they woke up, they noticed that they could not move; the reason was that during the night the native

Oreillons,[45] to whom the two ladies had denounced them, had tied them down with cords made of bark. They were surrounded by about fifty Oreillons, completely nude, armed with arrows, clubs, and stone axes. Some were bringing a huge cauldron to boil; others were preparing spits; and all of them were chanting: "It's a Jesuit, it's a Jesuit; here's our revenge and here's a good meal; let's eat Jesuit, let's eat Jesuit."

"Dear Master, I warned you," Cacambo blurted out sadly, "that these two girls would bring us trouble."

Candide, seeing the cauldron and the spits, exclaimed, "We're definitely going to be roasted or boiled. Ah! What would Dr. Pangloss say, if he knew what the pure state of nature is really like? All is well they say; but I confess it's harsh to have lost Miss Cunégonde and to be skewered by Oreillons."

Cacambo never lost his head. "Don't give up hope yet," he said to the cheerless Candide. "I know a bit of the lingo of tribes like this; I'm going to speak to them."

"Remember to explain to them," added Candide, "that it's the height of inhumanity to cook human beings, and that it's not very Christian either."

"Gentlemen," said Cacambo, "you intend to eat a Jesuit today; that is appropriate; nothing is more just than to treat one's enemies in this way. Indeed, natural law teaches us to kill our neighbor, and that is how everyone behaves the whole world over. If we Europeans do not exercise our right to eat others, it is because we have other ingredients for a good meal. But you do not have the same resources. It certainly makes more sense to eat your enemies than to abandon the fruits of victory to crows and ravens. But gentlemen, you do not wish to eat your friends. You think you are going to put a Jesuit on the spit, but it is your defender, the enemy of your enemies, whom you are going to roast. As for myself, I was born in your country; this gentleman whom you see is my master; and far from being a Jesuit, he just killed a Jesuit! He is wearing the plunder, and that is the source of your mistake. To verify what I am telling you, take his robe, bring it to the first outpost of the kingdom of the *Padres*. Learn for yourselves if my master has not killed a Jesuit officer. It will not take long; you can always eat us later if you find that I have lied to you. But if I have

---

[45]"Oreillons" means big ears. In Garcilaso de la Vega's *Comentarios reales,* a work first published in 1609, Voltaire had read about a tribe of Indians in Peru who pierced and distended their ears. According to Vega, the members of this tribe had a propensity for nudity, sodomy with monkeys, and cannibalism. On Voltaire's borrowings from Vega, see Richard Brooks, "Voltaire and Garcilaso de la Vega," *Studies on Voltaire and the Eighteenth Century,* vol. 30, 1964, 189–204.

spoken the truth, you are too familiar with the principles of international justice, morality, and law not to spare our lives."

The Oreillons found this speech very reasonable. They commissioned two leaders to determine the truth with haste. The two deputies carried out their mission with precision and soon came back with the good news. The Oreillons untied their two prisoners, made all kinds of apologies, offered them girls, gave them refreshments, and escorted them up to the boundary of their state, shouting joyfully, "He's not a Jesuit, he's not a Jesuit!"

Candide could not stop admiring the cause of his deliverance. "What a people!" he kept saying. "What men! What morals! If I hadn't been lucky enough to stick a sword through the body of Miss Cunégonde's brother, I would have been eaten without mercy. But it turns out the pure state of nature is good, because I only had to show these people I wasn't a Jesuit, and they treated me with enormous kindness."

CHAPTER 17

Arrival of Candide and his valet in the country of Eldorado,[46] and what they saw there

When they were at the Oreillons' border, Cacambo said to Candide, "You see, this hemisphere is no better than the other. Listen, let's take the shortest route back to Europe."

"How can we?" said Candide. "And where would we go? If I go back to my country, the Bulgars and Abars are slaughtering everyone. If I return to Portugal, I'll be burned. If we stay here, we run the risk of being put on a spit. And how can I bring myself to leave the part of the world where Miss Cunégonde lives?"

"Let's head for Cayenne," said Cacambo. "There we can find some Frenchmen who travel all over the world. They'll be able to help. Perhaps God will have pity on us."

It was not easy to get to Cayenne. They had a good idea, more or less, of the direction to take; but everywhere mountains, rivers, cliffs, bandits, and savages blocked their way. Their horses died of fatigue; their provisions were used up; they lived on wild fruits for a whole month. At last they found themselves by a little river, fringed with coconut trees, which nourished their lives and hopes.

---

[46]The myth of Eldorado, a land of gold, fascinated Europeans since the discovery of the New World.

Cacambo, whose advice was always as good as the old woman's, said to Candide: "We can't go any further, we've walked enough. I see an empty canoe on the shore. Let's fill it with coconuts, jump into this little bark, and drift with the current. A river always leads to some inhabited place. If we don't find something we like, we'll at least find something new."

"Let's go," said Candide, "and may Providence guide us."

They drifted for several miles between banks that were sometimes fertile, sometimes barren, sometimes level, sometimes steep. The river grew steadily broader, and eventually vanished under a vault of terrifying rocks that soared into the sky. The two travelers had the boldness to abandon themselves to the currents below this vault. The river narrowed at this point and carried them along with horrifying speed and noise. After twenty-four hours, they saw daylight again, but their canoe broke apart against the reefs. They had to crawl from rock to rock for three miles. Finally, they discovered a vast horizon trimmed by unscalable mountains. The lowlands were cultivated for pleasure as well as profit. Everywhere the useful was combined with the pleasing. The roads were covered, or rather embellished, with elegantly shaped carriages made from a shiny material, carrying men and women of extraordinary beauty, drawn swiftly by large red sheep that surpassed in speed the finest horses of Andalusia, Tetuan, and Mequinez.

"Here at last," said Candide, "is a country that is better than Westphalia."

He and Cacambo stepped into the first village they encountered. Some of the village children, covered with bits of golden brocade, were playing quoits near the village gate. Our two men from the other world watched them with interest. Their quoits were rather large rounded objects, yellow, red, and green, which sparkled brilliantly. Out of curiosity the travelers picked some up: gold, emeralds, rubies, of which the smallest would have been the greatest ornament of the Mogul's throne.

"No doubt about it," said Cacambo, "these youngsters playing quoits are the children of the King of this land."

Just then the village schoolteacher appeared to call the children back to school.

"There," said Candide, "is the tutor to the royal family."

The little beggars promptly stopped playing, leaving their quoits on the ground, along with their other playthings. Candide picked them up, ran after the instructor, and humbly presented them to him, using signs to tell him that the royal children had forgotten their gold and precious stones. The village schoolteacher smiled and threw them to the ground, looked briefly at Candide's face with surprise, and went on his way.

The travelers did not fail to keep the gold, rubies, and emeralds. "Where are we?" exclaimed Candide. "The children of kings must be well educated here because they are taught to despise gold and jewels." Cacambo was as surprised as Candide. Next they arrived at the first house in the village. It was built like a European palace. A throng of people crowded around the door, and even more were inside. A delightful music was audible, and a delicious odor of cooking filled the air. Cacambo walked up to the door and heard them speaking Peruvian. It was his mother tongue, for everyone knows that Cacambo was born in Tucuman, in a village where Peruvian was the only language.

"I'll act as your interpreter," he said to Candide. "Let's enter, this is an inn."

Two waiters and two waitresses, dressed in gold cloth, with their hair bound up in ribbons, invited them to be seated at the common dining table. They served four tureens of soup, each garnished with two parrots, a boiled condor weighing two hundred pounds, two savory roasted monkeys, three hundred round-billed hummingbirds on one platter, and six hundred straight-billed hummingbirds on another, exquisite stews, delicious pastries; and everything served on platters of a sort of rock crystal. The waiters and waitresses poured several liqueurs made from sugar cane. The guests were mostly merchants and coachmen, all extremely polite, who asked Cacambo a few questions with unintrusive discretion, and answered his own questions with the utmost clarity.

When the meal was over, Cacambo, like Candide, thought he was paying his bill amply by dropping on the table two of those large pieces of gold he had picked up. The host and hostess burst out laughing and slapped their knees for a long time. Finally, they became serious.

"Gentlemen," said the host, "we can easily see that you are foreigners; we are not accustomed to seeing any around here. Forgive us for laughing when you offered to pay us with stones from our highways. You obviously have none of our currency, but you do not need it to dine here. All inns established for the convenience of trade are paid for by the Government.[47] You have dined poorly here because this is a poor village; but everywhere else you'll be given the reception you deserve."

Cacambo explained to Candide all of the host's remarks, and Candide heard them with the same wonder and amazement that his friend Cacambo showed in translating them.

---

[47]Eldorado is thus a commercial society in which the state assists businessmen. Eldorado, unlike most other European visions of utopia up to this time, is a delight for the material self, filled with sumptuous food and luxury items.

"What is this country," they asked each other, "unknown to the rest of the world, and where the whole arrangement of Nature is so different from our own?"

"This is probably the country where all is well," Candide observed, "for it is absolutely necessary that one such country exist. And in spite of what Dr. Pangloss used to say, I often observed that everything was for the worst in Westphalia."

CHAPTER 18

What they saw in the land of Eldorado

Cacambo expressed his curiosity to his host, and the host said to him, "I am a very ignorant man, and am content to be so; but we do have an old gentleman, retired from the royal court, who is the most learned person in the kingdom, and the most communicative."

Without delay he brought Cacambo to the old man's house. Candide was merely the supporting actor now and accompanied his valet. They went into a very simple home, for the door was only silver, and the interior paneling merely gold, though designed with so much taste that the richest paneling could not surpass it. The lobby floor, it is true, was encrusted only with rubies and emeralds, but the harmonious pattern in which everything was arranged compensated for this extreme simplicity.

The old man received the two foreigners on a sofa stuffed with hummingbird feathers. He offered them liqueurs in diamond vases; after which he satisfied their curiosity in these terms.

"I am a hundred and seventy-two years old, and my late father, who was Master of the Royal Stables, told me about the astounding revolutions in Peru that he had witnessed. The kingdom we are in is the original homeland of the Incas, who unwisely left it to go out and make foreign conquests, and who ended up being destroyed by the Spanish.

"More wisdom was shown by some princes who remained here in their native land. They commanded, with the nation's consent,[48] that no inhabitant of our little kingdom would ever leave it; and this rule has preserved our innocence and our happiness. The Spanish have some vague knowledge of this country, which they call *El Dorado,* and an English lord named Raleigh even came close to it about a hundred years ago. But since

---

[48]This is the only evidence for the form of government in Eldorado. It seems to be a constitutional monarchy: the King governs with the approval of the nation or its representatives.

we are surrounded by impassable mountains and precipices, we have so far been safe from the greed of European nations, which have an incredible passion for the stones and mud of our land and would murder every one of us to get some."

The conversation continued for a long time. It turned on the form of government, the morals, the women, the public entertainments, the arts. Finally, Candide, who always had a taste for metaphysics, inquired through Cacambo if the country had a religion.

The old man blushed slightly.

"How could you ever think we did not? Do you take us for ungrateful wretches?"

Cacambo humbly asked what the religion of Eldorado was. The old man blushed again.

"Is there more than one religion?" he said. "We have, I believe, the same religion as everyone else. We worship God from morning to night."

"Do you worship just one God?" asked Cacambo, who continued to translate Candide's uncertainties.

"I see no reason," said the old man, "to believe in two, three, or four. I must say that people from your world ask very odd questions."

Candide did not tire of interrogating the good old man through Cacambo. He wanted to know how one prayed to God in Eldorado.

"We do not pray at all," said the good and respectable sage; "we have nothing to ask him for; he has given us everything we need, and we thank him constantly."

Candide was curious to see the priests. He asked where they were. The kindly oldtimer smiled.

"My friends," said he, "we are all priests. The King and all the heads of families solemnly chant the psalms of thanksgiving every morning, and five or six thousand citizens sing along with them."

"What! You have no monks who lecture, debate, govern, conspire, and burn people who don't agree with them?"

"We would be crazy if we did," said the old man. "Everyone here has the same beliefs, and we do not understand what your monks are for."

Candide was in ecstasy at these remarks, and said to himself, "This is very different from Westphalia and the Baron's chateau. If our friend Pangloss had seen Eldorado, he would have stopped asserting that the castle of Thunder-ten-tronckh was the best thing on earth. Travel is certainly instructive."

After this long conversation, the kindly oldtimer had a carriage harnessed with six sheep and had twelve of his servants take the two travelers to the court.

"Forgive me," he said to them, "if my age deprives me of the honor of accompanying you. The King will give you a reception that will not disappoint you, and I am sure you will excuse us for any customs that happen to displease you."

Candide and Cacambo climbed into the carriage. The six sheep flew off, and in less than four hours they arrived at the royal palace, located on the edge of the capital city. The portal was two hundred and twenty feet high and a hundred wide. It is impossible to describe the materials it was made of, but it was obvious that it was vastly superior to those stones and sand we call gold and jewels.

Twenty beautiful girls of the palace guard met Candide and Cacambo as they descended from the carriage, escorted them to the baths, and dressed them in robes spun from hummingbird down. Then the Grand Lords and Ladies of the Crown walked them to His Majesty's apartment, passing between two lines of a thousand musicians each, as was the custom. As they approached the throne room, Cacambo asked a Grand Officer how they were supposed to show respect for His Majesty. By falling on their knees or flat on their stomachs? By putting their hands on their heads or behind their backs? By licking the dust off the floor? In short, what was the ceremony?

"The custom," said the Grand Officer, "is to embrace the King and kiss him on both cheeks."

Candide and Cacambo hugged His Majesty, who received them with the utmost grace and politely invited them to have supper with him later. In the meantime, they were shown the city: the public buildings rising to the clouds; the open markets decorated with countless columns; the fountains of clear water, the fountains of rose water, and the fountains of liqueurs made from sugar cane, which flowed continuously in great public squares that were paved with a kind of precious stone that gave off the scent of cloves and cinnamon. Candide asked to see the law courts; they told him that none existed and that trials never occurred. He inquired whether they had prisons, and the answer was no. What surprised him even more, and gave him the most pleasure, was the Palace of Science, in which he visited a gallery, two thousand paces long, filled with instruments for mathematics and physics.

After spending the whole afternoon touring about one-thousandth of the city, they returned to the Palace. Candide sat down to supper with His Majesty, his valet Cacambo, and several ladies. Never did they taste better food, and never did they encounter a more urbane host than His Majesty. Cacambo explained the King's witticisms to Candide, and they were witty even in translation. Of all the astonishing things Candide saw and heard, this was by no means the least astonishing.

They spent a month in this retreat. Candide never stopped saying to Cacambo: "It's true, my friend, and I'll repeat it: the castle where I was born doesn't compare to the land we're in now. But still, Miss Cunégonde isn't here, and you probably have a mistress yourself somewhere in Europe. If we stay here, we'll just be like everyone else, whereas if we return to our world, even with only twelve sheep loaded with stones from Eldorado, we'll be richer than all the kings put together. We won't have to be afraid of inquisitors, and we'll easily be able to rescue Miss Cunégonde."

This speech pleased Cacambo. People so much like to roam around, and then show off at home and brag about what they have seen in their travels, that the two happy men resolved to be happy no longer, and to ask His Majesty for permission to leave.

"You are doing a foolish thing," the King said to them. "I know that my country is insignificant, but when one is tolerably well off somewhere one ought to remain there. I certainly have no right to confine foreigners; such tyranny is inconsistent with our customs and with our laws.[49] All men are free. You may leave at will, but the way out is very difficult. It is impossible to go against the swift currents which miraculously brought you here and which flow through the vaults of rock. The mountains surrounding my entire realm are ten thousand feet high and as straight as walls. Each one is more than twenty-five miles wide, and the only way down the other side is over vertical cliffs. Since you are absolutely determined to leave, however, I will order the Royal Engineers to design something that can transport you comfortably. When you have been conveyed to the other side of the mountains, no one will be able to accompany you beyond; for my subjects have sworn never to leave this retreat, and they are too wise to break their vows. But ask me for anything else you desire."

"We ask of Your Majesty," said Cacambo, "only a few sheep loaded with provisions, and some of the stones and mud of your country."

The King laughed. "I do not comprehend," he said, "the taste you Europeans have for our yellow mud; but take as much as you want, and may it bring you well-being."

He promptly gave orders to his engineers to make a machine to hoist these two extraordinary men out of the kingdom. Three thousand expert physicists worked on it; it was ready in two weeks and cost no more than

---

[49]An allusion to Frederick the Great's treatment of Voltaire in 1753, when he would not allow him to leave Germany after a lengthy visit.

twenty million pounds sterling in the local currency. Candide and Cacambo were placed in the machine. There were two large red sheep, saddled and bridled, for them to ride after they traversed the mountains, as well as twenty pack sheep loaded with provisions, thirty carrying gifts of the country's most curious items, and fifty loaded with gold, precious stones, and diamonds. The king tenderly embraced the two vagabonds.

It was a wonderful spectacle to see their departure and the ingenious way in which they and their sheep were hauled over the mountains. The physicists took leave of them after setting them down safely, and Candide's only aim and desire now was to present his sheep to Miss Cunégonde.

"We have enough to pay off the Governor of Buenos Aires," he said, "if Miss Cunégonde can be purchased. Let's head for Cayenne, let's set sail, and we will see what kingdom we can buy."

CHAPTER 19

What happened to them in Surinam, and how Candide became acquainted with Martin

The first day was quite pleasant for our two travelers. They were encouraged by the idea that they possessed more treasure than all of Asia, Europe, and Africa combined. Candide was elated, and carved the name of Cunégonde on trees. On the second day, two of their sheep sank into a swamp and were buried with their cargo; two other sheep died of fatigue a few days after that; seven or eight perished of hunger in a desert; others fell off some cliffs a few days later. Finally, after a hundred days of travel, they had only two sheep left.

Candide said to Cacambo, "My friend, you see how the riches of this world are ephemeral; nothing is solid but virtue and the happiness of seeing Miss Cunégonde again."

"I agree," said Cacambo, "but we still have two sheep with more treasure than the King of Spain will ever have, and I see in the distance a city that I suspect is Surinam, which belongs to the Dutch. We are at the end of our troubles and the beginning of our happiness."

As they approached the town they saw a Negro stretched out on the ground, wearing only a pair of blue linen trunks that were half torn away. The poor man was missing his left leg and right hand.[50]

---

[50]The use of African slaves in the European colonies of America rose dramatically in the eighteenth century. After he had already completed a draft of *Candide*, Voltaire was

"Oh my God!" Candide said to him in Dutch. "What are you doing in this horrible condition, my friend?"

"I'm waiting for my master, Mr. Vanderdendur, the famous merchant," replied the Negro.

"Was it Mr. Vanderdendur," asked Candide, "who treated you this way?"

"Yes, sir," said the Negro, "it's normal. They give us one pair of linen trunks twice a year as our only clothing. When we work in the sugar mills and catch our fingers in the grinder, they cut off our hand. When we try to escape, they cut off our leg.[51] I've had both punishments. It is at this price that you eat sugar in Europe. Yet, when my mother sold me for ten Patagonian crowns on the coast of Guinea, she said to me, 'My dear child, pray to our charms, worship them forever, they will bring you happiness. You have the honor of becoming a slave to our Masters, the whites, and by doing so, you are making your parents rich.' Alas, I don't know if they became rich, but I certainly didn't. Dogs, monkeys, and parrots are a thousand times less miserable than we are. The Dutch sorcerers who converted me tell me every Sunday that we are all children of Adam, whites and blacks. I'm no genealogist, but if these preachers are right, we're all cousins. Now you have to admit that you can't treat your relatives more horribly than this."

"Oh Pangloss!" exclaimed Candide. "You had no idea this abomination existed. That does it; I have to renounce your optimism after all."

"What's optimism?" asked Cacambo.

"Alas!" said Candide, "it's the mania for insisting that all is well when one is suffering."

And he shed tears as he looked at the Negro. He was still crying when he entered Surinam.

The first thing he did was to inquire whether there was a ship in the harbor that could sail to Buenos Aires. The person they asked happened to be a Spanish captain who offered to make an honest deal with them and arranged to meet them later at an inn. Candide and the trusty Cacambo went to wait for him with their two sheep.

Candide, who wore his heart on his sleeve, told the Spaniard about all his adventures, and revealed that he wished to carry off Miss Cunégonde.

"The last thing I would do is take you to Buenos Aires," said the Captain. "I would be hanged, and so would you. The lovely Cunégonde is His Lordship's favorite mistress."

---

moved by descriptions of the plantations to modify the text so as to add this scene condemning slavery.

[51]The abuse of slaves in the manner described here was in fact common. See André Morize's discussion in *Candide: édition critique* (Paris: Droz, 1931), 128–29.

This was a lightning bolt for Candide. He wept for a long time. Finally, he drew Cacambo aside.

"Here's what you must do, my dear friend. Each of us has in his pockets five or six million worth of diamonds. You're more clever than I am. Go get Miss Cunégonde in Buenos Aires. If the Governor makes any trouble, give him a million. If he doesn't give in to that, offer him two. You never killed an inquisitor, they won't be suspicious of you. I'll fit out another boat and go to Venice and wait for you. It's a free country where you don't have to be afraid of Bulgars or Abars or Jews or inquisitors."

Cacambo approved of this wise resolution. He was in distress at having to separate from such a good master, who had become his intimate friend. But the pleasure of being useful to him outweighed the pain of leaving him. They embraced and shed tears. Candide urged him not to forget the old woman. Cacambo left the very next day. He was a very fine man, that Cacambo.

Candide stayed on in Surinam, waiting until another Captain could take him to Italy with the two sheep he had left. He hired servants and bought everything he needed for a long voyage. Finally, Mr. Vanderdendur, proprietor of a big ship, came to introduce himself.

"How much do you want," Candide asked this man, "to take me straight to Venice, me, my men, my baggage, and those two sheep?"

The owner suggested ten thousand piastres. Candide immediately accepted.

"Ho ho," said the prudent Vanderdendur to himself, "this foreigner gives up ten thousand piastres in a second! He must be very rich."

Then, returning a moment later, he declared that he could not embark for less than twenty thousand.

"All right, you shall be paid," said Candide.

"Hey," the merchant said under his breath, "this man gives twenty thousand piastres as easily as he gives ten."

He came back again and said that he could not transport him to Venice for less than thirty thousand piastres.

"Then you will get thirty thousand," Candide replied.

"Ah ha," the Dutch merchant said to himself again, "thirty thousand piastres mean nothing to this man. Without any doubt, the two sheep are carrying immense treasures. Let us leave it as it stands. We will collect our thirty thousand piastres first, and then we will see."

Candide sold two little diamonds, the smaller of which was worth more than all the money the merchant demanded. He paid in advance. The two sheep were loaded on board. Candide followed on a small boat in order to join the ship in the harbor. The merchant seized the moment, raised the sail, and cut loose with a favorable wind. Candide, bewildered and stupefied, soon lost sight of him.

"Alas!" he cried out. "There's a trick worthy of the Old World."

He returned to shore, sunk in misery, for after all he had lost enough to make the fortune of twenty monarchs. He rushed to the house of a Dutch judge, and since he was a bit excited, he knocked rudely on the door. He entered, related his adventure, and shouted a bit louder than was necessary. The judge began by fining him ten thousand piastres for the noise he had made. Then he listened patiently, promised to review the case as soon as the merchant returned, and charged him another ten thousand piastres for the consultation.

These measures completed Candide's despair. He had, it is true, experienced other misfortunes a thousand times more painful, but the heartless character of the judge, and of the man who robbed him, amplified his bitterness and plunged him into a black melancholy. The viciousness of men appeared to him in all its ugliness, and he fed exclusively on thoughts of gloom. Finally, when a French ship was about to leave for Bordeaux, he took a cabin at a fair price, and since he no longer had any sheep laden with diamonds to bring with him, he announced in town that he would pay the fare, board, and two thousand piastres to any honest man who wished to make the voyage with him, on condition that this man should be the most disgusted with his lot and the most miserable in the province.

A throng of applicants appeared that an entire fleet could not have held. Candide wished to select the most promising candidates; he picked out about twenty persons who seemed sociable enough and all claimed to be the most qualified. He assembled them in his inn and gave them supper, on condition that each one swear to tell his story faithfully. He would choose the one who seemed to deserve the most pity and to have the strongest claim to being unhappy with his lot; the others would receive some smaller reward.

The session lasted until four in the morning. As he listened to all their adventures, Candide remembered what the old woman had told him on the way to Buenos Aires, and the wager she had made that there was no one on board who had not experienced great misfortunes. He thought of Pangloss at each tale he heard.

"That Pangloss," he said, "would be hard put to defend his system now. I wish he were here. Obviously, if all is well, it's in Eldorado and not in the rest of the world."

Finally, he decided in favor of a poor scholar who had worked in the bookstores of Amsterdam for ten years. He came to the conclusion that there was no profession on earth with which a man could be more disgusted.[52]

This scholar, who was in fact a decent man, had been robbed by his wife, beaten by his son, and abandoned by his daughter, who had eloped with a Portuguese. He had just been deprived of the little job that barely supported him, and the preachers of Surinam were persecuting him because they took him to be a Socinian.[53] In truth, the others were at least as unfortunate as he, but Candide hoped that the scholar would relieve his boredom during the voyage. All his other rivals thought that Candide was doing them a great injustice, but he appeased them by giving them a hundred piastres each.

CHAPTER 20

What happened to Candide and Martin at sea

The old scholar, whose name was Martin, thus set out for Bordeaux with Candide. They had both seen much, and suffered much; and even if the ship had been scheduled to sail from Surinam to Japan by the Cape of Good Hope, they would have had enough material to discuss moral and physical evil throughout the entire voyage.

Yet, Candide had one great advantage over Martin: he still hoped to see Miss Cunégonde again, while Martin had nothing to hope for. Besides, he still had some gold and diamonds. Even though he had lost a hundred big red sheep packed with the greatest treasures of the earth, and even though he was still tormented by the Dutch merchant's trickery, when he thought about what he still had in his pockets, and when he spoke of Cunégonde, especially after a good meal, he still leaned toward the system of Pangloss.

"But you, Mister Martin," said he to the scholar, "what do you think of all this? What's your conception of moral and physical evil?"

"Sir," replied Martin, "my priests accused me of being a Socinian; but the truth is that I am a Manichean."[54]

---

[52]Publishing was a cutthroat business in the eighteenth century. Voltaire, who had many quarrels with publishers, expresses his bitterness here.

[53]A religious rationalist who denies the divinity of Christ, the Trinity, and original sin.

[54]A heresy dating back to the third century A.D., Manicheanism was a belief that two principles, one good, the other evil, contended as equals for mastery of the universe. The Catholic Church denied that a powerful evil force necessarily kept goodness in check.

"You're joking," said Candide, "there are no more Manicheans in the world."

"There's myself," said Martin. "I don't know what to do about it, but I can't think any other way."

"The Devil must be inside your body," said Candide.

"He's so involved in the affairs of this world," said Martin, "that he may well be in my body and everywhere else too. But I confess that when I survey this globe, or rather this tiny ball, I think that God has abandoned it all to some evil being—except of course Eldorado. Very rarely have I seen a town that did not wish for the destruction of the next town, or a family that did not seek to exterminate some other family. Everywhere the weak hate the powerful in whose presence they slither, and the strong look after the weak like sheep to be fleeced and slaughtered. A million assassins in uniform, roaming from one end of Europe to the other, murder and pillage with discipline in order to earn their daily bread, and no profession confers more honor. And in those towns that seem to enjoy peace and where the arts flourish, the jealousies, cares, and anxieties that devour men are greater than the scourges suffered by a besieged city. Secret distress is much worse than public misfortune. In short, I've seen enough, and suffered enough, to be a Manichean."

"Yet there's some good," replied Candide.

"That may be," said Martin, "but I never saw it."

In the middle of this discussion, they heard the sound of cannon growing louder at every moment. Every one reached for his spyglass and saw two ships fighting about three miles away. The wind brought them both so close to the French ship that they had the pleasure of watching the fight in comfort. Finally one of the two ships assaulted the other with a broadside so low and accurate that it sank toward the bottom. Candide and Martin clearly discerned about a hundred men on the deck of the sinking vessel; they all raised their hands to heaven and wailed in terror. A moment later they were all swallowed up.

"Well," said Martin, "that's how men treat each other."

"It's true," said Candide, "there's something diabolical in this affair."

As he uttered these words he made out something bright red swimming toward the ship. They launched a lifeboat to see what it could be: it was one of his sheep. Candide's joy at regaining his one sheep was greater than his grief when he had lost a hundred of them packed with big diamonds from Eldorado.

The French Captain soon discovered that the Captain of the attacking ship was Spanish and that the Captain of the submerged ship was a Dutch pirate; it was, in fact, the same who had robbed Candide. The immense riches stolen by that scoundrel were buried with him in the sea, and only one of the sheep survived.

"You see," Candide said to Martin, "sometimes crime is punished. That villainous Dutch merchant got the fate he deserved."

"Yes," said Martin, "but was it necessary for the ship's passengers to perish as well? God punished the deceiver, the Devil drowned the others."

Meanwhile the French and Spanish vessels continued on their way, and Candide continued his conversations with Martin. They debated for two weeks in a row, and at the end of this period they were no more advanced than on the first day. Nevertheless, they were talking, communicating ideas, and consoling one another. Candide caressed his sheep.

"Since I have found you again, I may well find Miss Cunégonde again too."

CHAPTER 21

How Candide and Martin theorized as they approached the coast of France

At last they sighted the coast of France.

"Have you been in France before, Mister Martin?" asked Candide.

"Yes," said Martin, "I have traversed many of the provinces. There are some where half the inhabitants are insane, some where the people are not to be trusted, some where they are quite gentle and rather ignorant, and others where they act like dandies all the time; and in all of them the principal occupation is lovemaking, the second is slandering, and the third is saying stupid things."

"But Mister Martin, have you ever seen Paris?"

"Yes, I have seen Paris. It has people in all of the above categories. It's a chaos, it's a mob in which everyone is seeking pleasure and in which almost no one finds it, at least so far as I could see. I did not stay there long. When I arrived I was robbed of all I had by pickpockets at the Saint-Germain fair. I was arrested myself as a thief and did a week in prison, and after that I became a printer's proofreader in order to earn enough to return to Holland on foot. I met the low-life of scribblers, the low-life of conspirators, and the low-life of convulsionaries.[55] They say there are some very polite people in that city; I wish it were true."

"As for me, I'm not at all curious to see France," said Candide. "You can easily understand that when someone has spent a month in Eldorado,

---

[55]The members of a Catholic sect called Jansenism sometimes manifested their religious ecstasy in group convulsions. Voltaire's brother Armand was one of them.

nothing else on earth is appealing any more, except Miss Cunégonde. I am going to wait for her in Venice. We will cross France to get to Italy. Will you join me?"

"Very gladly," Martin said. "They say that Venice is a good place only for the Venetian nobles but that they also receive foreigners well when they have a lot of money. I don't have any, but you do; I will follow you anywhere."

"By the way," said Candide, "do you think that the earth was originally a sea, as it states in that fat book belonging to the ship's Captain?"[56]

"I believe nothing of the sort," said Martin, "any more than all the other pipe dreams that people have been selling recently."

"But then for what purpose was the earth formed?" asked Candide.

"To drive us crazy," replied Martin.

"Aren't you amazed," Candide went on, "by the story I told you about those two girls who were in love with the monkeys in the land of the Oreillons?"

"Not at all," Martin said, "I see nothing bizarre in that passion. I have seen so many extraordinary things that nothing is extraordinary any more."

"Do you think," Candide asked, "that men have always massacred each other as they do today, and that they have always been liars, cheaters, traitors, ingrates, brigands, weaklings, deserters, cowards, enviers, gluttons, drunks, misers, profiteers, predators, slanderers, perverts, fanatics, hypocrites, and morons?"

"Do you think," Martin said, "that hawks have always eaten pigeons when they found any?"

"Yes, of course," said Candide.

"Well," said Martin, "if hawks have always had the same character, why do you expect that men have changed theirs?"

"Oh!" said Candide, "that's very different, for free will . . . "

As they were theorizing, they arrived in Bordeaux.

CHAPTER 22

What happened to Candide and Martin in France

Candide stopped in Bordeaux only as long as it took to sell a few stones from Eldorado and to hire a fine carriage with two seats, for he could no longer do without his philosopher, Martin. He was very upset, however,

---

[56]The big book could be the Bible but is more likely Buffon's *Histoire naturelle* (1750–70) or De Brosses's *Histoire des navigations aux terres australes* (1756)—both developed the theory that the earth was originally covered entirely by water.

that he had to leave his sheep. He left it with the Bordeaux Academy of Sciences, which organized its annual essay competition around the question of why this sheep's wool was red. The prize was awarded to a scholar from the North, who proved by A plus B minus C divided by Z that the sheep had to be red, and that it would die of the sheep-pox.

Meanwhile, all the travelers Candide met in the inns along the road said to him, "We are going to Paris!" This general eagerness finally made him want to see the capital; it was not far off the route to Venice anyway.

He entered through the Faubourg Saint-Marceau and thought he was in the ugliest village of Westphalia.

Scarcely was Candide in his hotel when he was struck by a mild illness caused by his fatigue. As he had an enormous diamond on his finger, and people had noticed a prodigiously heavy trunk among his belongings, he immediately had at his bedside two doctors whom he had not summoned, several intimate friends who would not leave him, and two pious women who kept his soup warm.

Martin said, "I remember being sick too during my first trip to Paris. I was a very poor man, so I had no friends, no pious ladies, no doctors, and I got better."

However, with the aid of medicines and bloodlettings, Candide's illness grew serious. A parish priest came and sweetly asked for a note payable to the bearer in the next world.[57] Candide would have nothing to do with it. The pious ladies assured him it was the latest fashion. Candide answered that he was not a fashionable man. Martin wanted to throw the priest out the window. The cleric swore that he would never grant Candide a proper burial. Martin swore that he would properly bury the cleric if he kept on bothering them. The quarrel heated up. Martin took him by the shoulders and rudely threw him out, creating a great scandal that was duly noted in a police report.

Candide recovered, and throughout his convalescence he had very good company for supper. They played cards for high stakes. Candide was surprised that he never got any aces, and Martin was not surprised at all.

Among those who bestowed upon him the city's favors was a little Perigordian Abbé,[58] one of those fellows on the move who is always alert,

---

[57] A reference to the *billet de confession* — a theological oath that the clergy could demand of a dying person before performing the last rites. The *billets* were designed to combat the Jansenists, French Catholics with unorthodox views about grace and human nature. A dying person who refused to sign a *billet* was considered outside of the Church and ineligible for burial on hallowed ground.

[58] A member of the clergy from the region of Périgord in southwestern France.

obliging, assertive, flattering, solicitous, and who lies in wait for foreigners passing through, offering to tell them about the town's scandals and to obtain pleasures for them at any price. This man first took Candide and Martin to the theater. They were performing a new tragedy.[59] Candide was seated next to some highbrow critics. That did not prevent him from weeping at the perfectly acted scenes. One of the theorizers beside him said during the intermission:

"It is highly improper of you to weep. That actress is very bad, the actor playing opposite her is worse, and the play is even worse than the actors. The author does not know a word of Arabic, yet the scene takes place in Arabia. Moreover, he does not believe in innate ideas.[60] Tomorrow I will bring you twenty pamphlets against him."

"Sir,[61] how many plays do you have in France?" Candide asked the Abbé.

"Five or six thousand," replied the Abbé.

"That's a lot," said Candide. "How many of them are good?"

"Fifteen or sixteen," answered the other.

"That's a lot," said Martin.

Candide was very pleased by an actress who played Queen Elizabeth in a rather dull tragedy[62] that is still performed from time to time.

"I like that actress a lot," he said to Martin. "She resembles Miss Cunégonde. I would like to pay her my respects."

The Perigordian Abbé volunteered to take him to her house. Candide, raised in Germany, asked what the etiquette was and how one treated the Queen of England in France.

"It depends," said the Abbé. "In the provinces you take them to a hotel. In Paris, you show them more respect if they are attractive, and then you throw them into the public dump when they are dead."

"Queens in the public dump!" said Candide.

"Yes, that's how it is," said Martin. "The Abbé is right. I was in Paris when Miss Monime passed, as they say, from this life to the next. They refused to give her what these people call 'the rites of burial,' in other words, the right to rot with all the beggars of the neighborhood in a sordid cemetery. Her troupe buried her all alone at the corner of the Rue de

[59]In one of the manuscript versions of *Candide,* Voltaire indicated that the play being performed in this chapter was one of his own—*L'Orphelin de la Chine.*

[60]Leibniz and Descartes believed in innate ideas—that concepts inhere in the mind. Voltaire preferred John Locke, who argued that ideas were derived from sensations.

[61]Voltaire added the section beginning here in the 1761 edition. The end of the addition is noted later in the chapter.

[62]A reference to *Le Comte d'Essex* by Thomas Corneille (1625–1709). As a young man Voltaire first achieved fame through his plays and was considered to be the greatest dramatist since Corneille. In this chapter, Candide attends a double-feature and clearly prefers Voltaire to Corneille!

Bourgogne; it must have caused her extreme pain, for she always had a noble mind."[63]

"That was very impolite," said Candide.

"What do you expect?" said Martin. "These people are made that way. Imagine every possible contradiction, every possible inconsistency; you will find it in the government, in the courts, in the churches, in the plays of this odd nation."

"Is it true that people in Paris always laugh?" asked Candide.

"Yes," said the Abbé, "but they are furious at the same time; for here people complain about everything with great bursts of laughter; they even laugh while committing the most detestable crimes."

"Who was that fat pig," asked Candide, "who said so many nasty things about the play that made me weep, and about the actors who gave me so much pleasure?"

"He is an illness in human form," replied the Abbé, "who makes a living by saying nasty things about every play and every book. He hates anyone who becomes popular, just as eunuchs hate anyone who makes love. He is one of those serpents of the literary world who feed on filth and poison; he is a folliculator."

"What do you mean by *folliculator?*" asked Candide.

"A scribbler of worthless folios, a Fréron,"[64] said the Abbé.

Candide, Martin, and the Perigordian had this discussion on the stairway, as they watched the crowd file out of the theater.

"Even though I'm very impatient to see Miss Cunégonde again," said Candide, "I would still like to have supper with Miss Clairon,[65] for she seemed admirable to me."

The Abbé was not in a position to approach Miss Clairon, who received only good company.

"She is already engaged this evening," he said, "but I will have the honor of introducing you to another lady of distinction, and there you will come to know Paris as if you had been here over four years."

Candide was naturally curious and let himself be taken to the lady's home in the middle of the Faubourg Saint-Honoré. A group was busy

[63]In civil and church law, acting was a vile profession that stripped the actors of many rights, including the right to be buried in Christian cemeteries. Miss Monime is an allusion to Adrienne Lecouvreur (1690–1730), an actress whom Voltaire admired. She suffered excommunication and her body was disgracefully cast in a public dump. From the 1730s through the 1760s, Voltaire pleaded for improvement of the status of actors.

[64]Elie Fréron (1719–76) was the most tenacious opponent of Voltaire and the philosophers of the Enlightenment. He published a critical review of *Candide* in his journal *Année littéraire*. The review is included in this volume.

[65]Miss Clairon (1723–1803), one of the great actresses of the Parisian stage.

playing faro there; twelve sad punters each had a small series of cards that plainly registered their bad luck. A deep silence reigned, the punters' faces were white, the banker's look was anxious, and the lady of the house, seated beside the pitiless banker, observed with the eyes of a lynx every doubling of the stakes, every multiple bet, which the players signified by bending their cards. She exposed cheaters strictly but politely, without anger, for fear of losing her clients. The Lady went by the name of the Marquise de Parolignac. Her fifteen-year-old daughter sat with the punters and winked at her mother to reveal the tricks these poor men were playing to repair the cruelties of chance. The Perigordian Abbé, Candide, and Martin entered. No one stood up, greeted them, or looked at them. Everyone was profoundly occupied with his cards.

"The Baroness of Thunder-ten-tronckh was more civil," thought Candide.

The Abbé, however, whispered in the ear of the Marquise. She stood up halfway and honored Candide with a gracious smile and Martin with a noble nod of the head. She arranged for Candide to sit and play cards. He lost fifty thousand francs in two rounds. Afterwards they had a very gay supper, and everyone was surprised that Candide was not disturbed by his loss. The lackeys said to each other, in their lackey language, "He must be some English Milord."

The supper was like most suppers in Paris: first silence; then a buzz of indistinguishable words; then jokes, insipid for the most part; inaccurate news; bad theory; a little politics, and a lot of slander. They even discussed new books.

"Has anyone seen," asked the Perigordian Abbé, "the novel by Monsieur Gauchat, Doctor of Theology?"[66]

"Yes," answered one of the guests, "but I could not finish it. We have a mass of trivial writings, but all of them put together do not match the triviality of Gauchat, Doctor of Theology. I am so nauseated by this multitude of detestable books that are swamping us that I have taken to playing faro."

"And the *Miscellaneous Essays* of Archdeacon T_____,[67] what do you think of them?" asked the Abbé.

"Oh!" said Madame de Parolignac, "that deadly bore! How fervently he says what everyone already knows! How heavily he discusses what is not worth the slightest notice! How he appropriates without wit the wit

---

[66]Gabriel Gauchat (1709–74) was a writer who defended orthodox Catholic views and repeatedly attacked Voltaire.

[67]Nicolas-Charles-Joseph Trublet (1697–1770), editor of the *Journal Chrétien,* was another enemy of Voltaire.

of others! How he spoils what he steals! How he disgusts me! But he will disgust me no more; after reading a few pages of the Archdeacon, I am through."

Seated at the table was a man of learning and taste who supported what the Marquise said. Next they discussed tragedies. The Lady asked why tragedies that were unreadable were sometimes performed on the stage. The man of taste explained very clearly that a play could be popular and worthless at the same time. With just a few words he proved that it was not enough to bring in one or two of those situations found in novels and that always seduce the audience. Rather, the writer had to be original without being bizarre; to be sublime, and always natural; to know the human heart and make it speak; to be a great poet without letting any character in the play appear to be a poet; to know the language perfectly, speak it purely, with a flowing harmony, and make it rhyme without ever straining the sense.

"Whoever does not observe each of these rules," he added, "can write one or two tragedies that receive applause at the theater, but he will never take a place among the ranks of good writers. There are very few good tragedies. Some are merely idylls in well-written and well-rhymed dialogues; others are political theories that put you to sleep, or endless declamations that repulse you; still others are the reveries of fanatics in a barbarous style, filled with disconnected notions, long orations to the gods — because the author has no idea how to communicate with men — false maxims, and pompous commonplaces."

Candide listened attentively to this speech and formed a great opinion of the speaker. Since the Marquise had taken care to seat him next to her, he leaned toward her and took the liberty of asking her who that man was who spoke so well.

"He is a scholar," said the Lady, "who does not play faro and whom the Abbé sometimes brings here for supper. He has a thorough knowledge of tragedies and books. He wrote a tragedy that was hissed in the theater and one book which no one has ever seen outside of his publisher's shop, except the copy that he presented to me."

"What a great man!" said Candide. "He is another Pangloss."

Then, turning toward him, he said, "Sir, no doubt you think that everything is for the best in the physical and moral worlds and that nothing could be otherwise than it is?"

"I, sir?" the scholar replied. "I think nothing of the sort. I find that we are wholly off course, that no one knows his station or his duties, what he is doing or should be doing, and that except during supper, when people are relatively gay and accommodating, the rest of the time is spent in trivial quarrels: Jansenists against Molinists,[68] men of parlement against men of the Church, men of letters against men of letters, courtiers against courtiers, financiers against the people, wives against their husbands, relatives against relatives: it is an eternal war."

Candide answered, "I've seen worse, but a wise man, who later had the misfortune to be hanged, taught me that such things are admirable: they are shadows in a beautiful picture."

"Your hanged teacher was mocking the world," said Martin. "Those shadows are horrible stains."

"It's men who make the stains," said Candide, "and they can't avoid it."

"Then it isn't their fault," said Martin.

Most of the card players, who grasped none of this exchange, were drinking. Martin continued to theorize with the scholars, and Candide recited part of his adventures to the Lady of the house.

After supper, the Marquise brought Candide into her boudoir and sat him down on a sofa.

"Well," she said, "are you still passionately in love with Miss Cunégonde of Thunder-ten-tronckh?"

"Yes, Madame," replied Candide.

The Marquise responded with a tender smile, "You answered me like a young man from Westphalia. A Frenchman would have said, 'It is true that I loved Miss Cunégonde, but when I see you, Madame, I fear that I am no longer in love with her.' "

"Alas! Madame," said Candide, "I will answer any way you want."

"Your passion for her," said the Marquise, "began when you picked up her handkerchief; I want you to pick up my garter."

"With all my heart," said Candide, and he picked it up.

"But I would like you to put it back on me," and Candide did so.

"Look at what a foreigner you are," said the Lady. "I sometimes force my Parisian lovers to languish for two weeks, but I am giving myself to you on the first night, because one should always bestow the favors of one's country on a young man from Westphalia."

The beauty had observed two enormous diamonds on the fingers of her young visitor, and she praised them so unselfishly that they passed from Candide's fingers to hers.

While returning home with his Perigordian Abbé, Candide felt some remorse at having been unfaithful to Miss Cunégonde. The Abbé took part in his sorrow. He had got only a small share of the fifty thousand

---

[68]Molinists were Jesuits who emphasized human free will. They violently opposed the Jansenists, who emphasized predestination and the total corruption of human nature.

francs Candide had lost in the card game, and of the value of the two diamonds that had been half given away by him and half extorted from him.
His scheme was to profit, as much as possible, from any advantages that
his association with Candide could provide. He spoke to him a great deal
about Cunégonde, and Candide told him that he would certainly ask the
lovely Lady to forgive him for his infidelity when he saw her again in
Venice.

The Perigordian multiplied his compliments and favors, and took a tender interest in everything Candide said, everything he did, everything he
wanted to do.[69]

"So you have a rendez-vous in Venice, sir?" he asked.

"Yes, Abbé," said Candide; "I absolutely must go find Miss Cunégonde."

Then, carried away by the pleasure of talking about his loved one, he
recounted, as was his habit, part of his adventures with that illustrious
Lady from Westphalia.

"I suppose," said the Abbé, "that Miss Cunégonde is highly cultivated
and writes charming letters."

"I never got any from her," said Candide. "Remember that when I was
driven from the castle because of my love for her, I couldn't write to her.
Then soon afterward, I learned she was dead. Then I found her again.
Then I lost her. And now I've sent a messenger to her, six thousand miles
away, and I'm waiting for his return."

The Abbé listened attentively, and then appeared to be lost in thought.
He soon took leave of the two foreigners after embracing them affec-
tionately. The next day, when Candide awoke, he received a letter composed as follows:

"Sir, my very dear lover, for a week I have been ill in this city. I know
that you are here. I would fly into your arms if I could move. I heard that
you had passed through Bordeaux. I left the faithful Cacambo and the
old woman there; they will soon follow me. The Governor of Buenos Aires
got everything from me he wanted, but I still have your heart. Come, the
sight of you will bring me back to life, or make me die of pleasure."

This charming, unexpected letter filled Candide with inexpressible joy,
and the illness of his dear Cunégonde struck him with grief. Torn
between these two sentiments, he took his gold and diamonds and drove
with Martin to the hotel where Miss Cunégonde was staying. He went
in, trembling with emotion, on the verge of sobbing, his heart pounding.
He tried to draw apart the bed curtains; he wanted more light.

[69]End of the section added in 1761.

"You mustn't do that," said the maid. "Light will kill her," and she abruptly closed the curtain.

"My dear Cunégonde," said Candide, weeping, "how are you feeling? If you can't see me, talk to me at least."

"She cannot speak, " said the maid.

But she drew out from the bed a plump hand, which Candide watered with tears for a long time, before filling it with diamonds. He also left a sack of gold on the armchair. In the midst of his raptures a police officer arrived, followed by the Perigordian Abbé and a squad of soldiers.

"Are these the foreigners under suspicion?" shouted the officer.

He immediately had them under guard, and ordered his henchmen to drag them to prison.

"This isn't the way they treated foreigners in Eldorado," said Candide.

"I'm more of a Manichean than ever," said Martin.

"But sir, where are you taking us?" said Candide.

"To a dungeon," said the officer.

Martin, who had regained his composure, figured out that the Lady claiming to be Cunégonde was a fraud, the Perigordian Abbé a fraud who had seized the chance to exploit Candide's innocence, and the police officer another fraud who could easily be bought off.

Rather than expose himself to the judicial process, Candide, enlightened by his advisor, and still eager to see the real Cunégonde, presented the officer with three little diamonds worth about three thousand pistoles[70] each.

"Ah sir!" said the man with the ivory baton, "even if you committed every crime imaginable, you're still the best man in the world. Three diamonds! Worth three thousand pistoles each! Sir! I would rather die than take you to jail. They are arresting all foreigners now, but leave everything to me. I have a brother at Dieppe, in Normandy. I'll take you there, and if you have a little diamond for him, he'll take care of you, just like me."

"And why are they arresting all foreigners?" asked Candide.

The Perigordian Abbé spoke up and said, "It's because a beggar from the region of Atrebatum fell under the influence of foolish ideas, and they were enough to inspire him to attempt a parricide, not like the one of May, 1610, but like the one of December, 1594, and like so many others attempted in other years, in other months, and by other beggars inspired by foolish ideas."[71]

[70]A Spanish gold coin.
[71]On January 5, 1757, Robert-François Damiens tried to stab Louis XV. Jean Châtel tried to kill Henry IV in 1594 and failed, unlike Ravaillac in 1610. Voltaire respected kingship and deplored all assassination attempts.

The officer then explained what it was all about.

"Oh, the monsters!" exclaimed Candide. "What! Such atrocities in a nation that dances and sings! Let me out of this country where monkeys attack tigers. I lived among bears in my country. Only in Eldorado did I live with human beings. In the name of God, officer, take me to Venice, where I am supposed to meet Miss Cunégonde.

"I can only take you to Lower Normandy," said the enforcer.

And he immediately removed the chains, announced that he had made a mistake, dismissed his men, and brought Candide and Martin to Dieppe, where he left them in the hands of his brother. There was a little Dutch ship in the harbor. The Norman, with the help of three other diamonds, developed into the most helpful of men and conducted Candide and his retinue onto the vessel bound for Portsmouth in England. It was not en route to Venice, but Candide felt that he had escaped from hell, and he confidently expected to resume the direction to Venice at the first opportunity.

CHAPTER 23

How Candide and Martin came to the shores of England, and what they saw there

"Oh, Pangloss! Pangloss! Oh, Martin! Martin! Oh, my darling Cunégonde! What is this world we live in?" cried Candide on the Dutch ship.

"Something insane, something abominable," replied Martin.

"You've lived in England. Are they as insane there as in France?"

"It's just a different kind of insanity," said Martin. "You know that these two countries have been at war over a few acres of snow in Canada, and that they are spending more on this lovely war than all of Canada is worth. As for whether there are more people in one country than another who ought to be put away, my limited intellect cannot say. I can only tell you that, in general, the people we are going to see are very melancholy."

As they were chatting, they arrived at Portsmouth. A large crowd of people covered the shore, looking out intently at a rather stout man who was on his knees, blindfolded, on the deck of a naval ship. Four soldiers stationed in front of this man peacefully fired three bullets each into his brain; and the entire crowd went away extremely satisfied.[72]

---

[72]On the eve of the Seven Years' War, Admiral John Byng was sent in 1755 to defend the island of Minorca against the French. Believing his force was insufficient, he fought a halfhearted engagement and left Minorca to the enemy. He was court-martialed and

"What's this all about?" asked Candide, "and what evil demon is exercising his empire everywhere?"

He asked about the identity of the large man who was just ceremoniously murdered.

"He's an Admiral," was the answer.

"And why kill this Admiral?"

"It's because," came the answer, "he didn't kill enough people. He was engaged in a battle with a French Admiral and was later judged to have kept too great a distance from the enemy."

"But," said Candide, "the French Admiral was as far from the English Admiral as the latter was from the former."

"That's incontestable," was the response. "But in this country they think it's good to kill an Admiral from to time to time, to encourage the others."

Candide was so stunned and shocked by what he saw and heard that he would not even set foot on land. He made a deal with the Dutch Captain (though the Captain could have robbed him like the one in Surinam) to take him to Venice without delay.

The Captain was ready two days later. They sailed along the coast of France. They passed within sight of Lisbon, and Candide shuddered. They entered the Straits of Gibraltar and the Mediterranean. At last they landed in Venice.

"God be praised," said Candide, embracing Martin. "This is where I will see the lovely Cunégonde again. I trust Cacambo as much as myself. All is well, all goes well, all is proceeding as best as it can."

CHAPTER 24

About Paquette and Brother Giroflée

As soon as he was in Venice, he looked for Cacambo in all the inns, all the cafés, and among all the ladies of pleasure, without finding him. He sent messengers every day to investigate every arriving boat, great and small: no news of Cacambo.

"What!" he said to Martin. "I've had time to go from Surinam to Bordeaux, from Bordeaux to Paris, from Paris to Dieppe, from Dieppe to Portsmouth, to sail along the coast of Portugal and Spain, to cross the entire Mediterranean, to spend several months in Venice—and the lovely

---

executed by a firing squad of marines on March 14, 1757. Voltaire had tried to intervene to save him.

Cunégonde still hasn't arrived! All I've encountered in her place is one pretentious strumpet and one Perigordian Abbé! Cunégonde is surely dead, and there is nothing left for me to do but die. Oh! It would have been better to stay in the paradise of Eldorado than to return to this accursed Europe. How right you are, my dear Martin! All is but illusion and catastrophe."

He fell into a black melancholy and attended none of the fashionable operas and entertainments of the carnival season. None of the ladies tempted him in the least.

Martin said to him: "You are really very naive if you think a half-breed valet, with five or six million in his pocket, is going to track down your mistress at the other end of the world and bring her to you in Venice. If he finds her, he'll take her for himself. If he doesn't find her, he'll take someone else. I advise you to forget about your valet Cacambo and your mistress Cunégonde."

Martin was not very comforting. Candide's melancholy grew worse, and Martin never stopped proving to him that there was little virtue and little happiness in the world, except perhaps in Eldorado, where nobody can go.

While they were discussing this important matter and waiting for Cunégonde, Candide noticed a young Theatine monk in the Piazza San Marco, arm in arm with a girl.[73] The monk looked fresh, plump, and vigorous; his eyes were brilliant, his manner confident, his head erect, his step proud. The girl was very pretty and she was singing. She gazed lovingly at him, and from time to time pinched his chubby cheeks.

"You'll at least admit," said Candide, "that those two are happy. Until now I've found nothing but miserable people throughout the inhabitable world, except Eldorado; but that girl and that monk, I'll bet they're very happy creatures."

"I'll bet they're not," said Martin.

"All we need to do is invite them to dinner," said Candide, "and we'll see if I'm wrong."

He immediately approached them, paid his respects, and invited them back to his inn to eat macaroni, Lombardy partridges, and caviar, and to drink wines from Montepulciano, Vesuvius, Cyprus, and Samos. The young lady blushed, the monk accepted the offer, and the girl followed, looking at Candide with surprised and confused eyes, which were dimmed by an occasional tear.

---

[73]Founded in 1524, the Theatines were a religious order devoted to combatting Protestantism and purifying the morality of the Catholic clergy.

Scarcely had she entered Candide's room when she said, "What! Master Candide does not recognize Paquette!"

At these words, Candide, who had not looked at her closely until then, because he was preoccupied with Cunégonde, said, "Alas! my poor child, so it's you, you who put Dr. Pangloss in the fine shape in which I saw him?"

"Alas! sir, I'm the one," said Paquette. "I see you know all about it. I heard about the terrible suffering inflicted on the household of the Baroness and on the fair Cunégonde. I swear to you, my fate has been no less unhappy. I was a pure and innocent girl when you saw me last. A Franciscan who was my confessor seduced me with ease. The consequences were horrible. I was forced to leave the castle shortly after the Baron had driven you out with great kicks in the behind. If a famous doctor hadn't taken pity on me, I would have died. For some time, as an expression of gratitude, I was this doctor's mistress. His wife was insanely jealous and used to beat me every day without mercy; she was a Fury. The doctor was the ugliest man alive, and I the unhappiest of all creatures, constantly beaten on account of a man I did not love.

"You understand, Sir, how dangerous it is for a nagging woman to be a doctor's wife. One day, enraged by his wife's complaints, he gave her some medicine for a slight cold; it was so effective that she died two hours later in horrible convulsions. Her relatives started criminal proceedings; he fled, and I was the one put in prison. My innocence would never have saved me if I had not been rather pretty. The judge set me free, on condition that he become the doctor's successor. I was soon replaced by another woman, driven away without any support, and obliged to continue that shameful profession which you men think is so pleasant but which is a miserable abyss for us. I came to Venice to exercise the profession. Oh! Sir, if only you could imagine what it's like to be obliged to caress equally an old merchant, a lawyer, a monk, a gondolier, an Abbé; to be exposed to every kind of insult and outrage; to be frequently reduced to borrowing a skirt so that some disgusting man can have the pleasure of lifting it; to be robbed by one man of what you've earned from another; to be blackmailed by officers of the law; and to have no future in view except an atrocious old age, a hospital, and the public dump—if you could imagine all this, you'd conclude that I am one of the most miserable creatures on earth."

Paquette thus opened her heart to the good Candide in a private room, in the presence of Martin, who said to Candide, "You see, I've already won half the bet."

Brother Giroflée had remained in the dining room and was having a drink while he waited for dinner.

"But," said Candide to Paquette, "you looked so gay, so happy, when I saw you; you were singing, you were caressing the monk with spontaneous affection; you seemed as happy then as you now claim to be miserable."

"Oh, Sir!" replied Paquette, "that's precisely one of the agonies of this profession. Yesterday I was robbed and beaten by an officer, and today I must appear to be in good spirits in order to give pleasure to a monk."

Candide did not wish to hear any more. He admitted that Martin was right. They sat down to eat with Paquette and the Theatine. The meal was quite amusing, and by the end, they were talking freely.

"Father," said Candide to the monk, "you seem to be enjoying a life that the whole world would envy. The flower of health blooms in your face; your features radiate with joy; you have a very pretty girl for recreation, and you seem content with your lot as a Theatine."

"Upon my word, Sir, I would like to see every Theatine at the bottom of the sea. A hundred times I have been tempted to set fire to the monastery and to run off and become a Turk. When I was fifteen my parents forced me to put on this detestable robe so they could leave more property to my accursed older brother, God confound him! Jealousy, discord, and rage fill the monastery. It is true that with a few bad sermons I bring in some money, half of which the Prior steals from me, half of which I use to procure women. But when I return to the monastery at night, I am ready to smash my head against the walls of the dormitory — and all the brothers feel the same."

Turning to Candide with his usual coolness, Martin said, "Well, haven't I won the whole bet?"

Candide gave two thousand piastres to Paquette and a thousand to brother Giroflée.

"I assure you," he said, "with that they will be happy."

"I know you're wrong," said Martin. "With those piastres you may even make them more unhappy than they ever were."

"Perhaps so," said Candide, "but one thing comforts me. I am learning that we often encounter people again whom we never thought we could find. It's quite possible that, having found my red sheep and Paquette again, I will also come across Cunégonde."

"If you do, I hope she makes you happy," said Martin, "but I strongly doubt she will."

"You're a hard man," said Candide.

"It's because I've lived," said Martin.

"But look at those gondoliers," said Candide. "Aren't they singing all day long?"

"You don't see them at home, with their wives and bratty children," said Martin. "The Doge[74] has his troubles, the gondoliers have theirs. It's true that on the whole, the fate of a gondolier is preferable to that of a Doge, but I think the difference is so small that it's not worth examining."

"People talk," said Candide, "about a Senator Pococurante,[75] who lives in the fine palace on the Brenta and who generously receives foreigners. They claim he's a man who has never known sorrow."

"I'd like to see such a rare specimen," said Martin.

Candide promptly sent word to ask Lord Pococurante's permission to see him the next day.

CHAPTER 25

A visit to Lord Pococurante, nobleman of Venice

Candide and Martin took a gondola down the Brenta and arrived at the noble Pococurante's palace. The gardens were ordered harmoniously and adorned with beautiful marble statues, and the palace itself was an architectural splendor. The master of the house, a man of sixty, and very wealthy, greeted his two curious visitors politely but with very little warmth, which disappointed Candide and impressed Martin.

First, two pretty and neatly attired girls served them cocoa whipped to a froth. Candide could not resist praising their beauty, grace, and dexterity.

"They are quite amusing creatures," said Senator Pococurante. "I sometimes take them to bed with me, for I am very tired of the ladies in town, their coquetries, their jealousies, their quarrels, their moods, their pettiness, their vanity, their foolishness, as well as the sonnets you have to compose or commission for them. But now these two girls are beginning to bore me too."

After the meal, Candide strolled through a long gallery and was surprised by the beauty of the paintings. He asked which master had painted the first two.

"They are by Raphael," said the Senator. "I bought them out of vanity at a high price a few years ago. People say they are the finest in Italy, but they do not give me any pleasure. The colors are too dark, the figures are not rounded enough and do not stand out enough, the draperies do

[74]Chief magistrate in Venice.
[75]Derived from Italian and meaning "caring little."

not look like real cloth at all.[76] In short, in spite of what they say, I do not consider them to be true imitations of Nature. I only like a painting when I think I am seeing Nature itself, but there are no paintings of this kind. I possess many paintings, but I do not look at them any more."

Pococurante had a concerto performed as they waited for dinner. Candide found the music delicious.

"That noise," said Pococurante, "may be amusing for a half hour, but if it goes on longer it tires everybody, though no one dares to admit it. The music of today is merely an art of performing difficult pieces, and what is merely difficult cannot be pleasing for very long.

"Perhaps I would like opera better, had they not discovered the formula for making it a revolting freak show. I have nothing against those who wish to see bad tragedies set to music, where the scenes are crudely written to introduce two or three ridiculous songs that show off an actress's windpipe. I have nothing against those who are willing or able to swoon with pleasure when a eunuch twitters the role of Caesar or Cato and struts awkwardly around the stage. But as for myself, I have long given up these trifles, which are now considered the glory of Italy, and for which Sovereigns pay so extravagantly."

Candide argued a little, but with discretion. Martin was entirely of the Senator's opinion.

They sat down to dine, and after an excellent dinner, they went into the library. Candide, seeing a superbly bound volume of Homer, complimented the most illustrious Lord on his good taste.

"Here," he said, "is a book that used to be a delight to the great Pangloss, the best philosopher in Germany."

"It has no such effect on me," said Pococurante coldly. "I was once under the delusion that reading gave me pleasure.[77] But that endless series of battles that are all alike, those gods who are always intervening without doing anything decisive, that Helen who is the cause of the war and who hardly plays a role in the story, that Troy which is forever besieged and never captured—all of this bores me to death. I have had opportunities to ask scholars if reading it bores them as

---

[76]Raphael was perhaps the greatest painter of the Italian Renaissance. The characteristics that Pococurante finds unsatisfactory are precisely the techniques in which Raphael excelled.

[77]After publishing *Candide*, Voltaire admitted that Pococurante represented a dark side of his own character. He sometimes fell into moods in which he could do nothing but denigrate the whole Western literary canon. All of the writers discussed in the following part of the text are classics that were considered essential reading for well-educated people in the eighteenth century.

much as it does me. All the sincere ones confessed that the book puts them to sleep but added that one must always have it in one's library as a monument to antiquity, like those rusty coins that cannot be spent."

"Your Excellency doesn't have the same opinion of Virgil?" said Candide.

"I grant," said Pococurante, "that the second, fourth, and sixth books of his *Aeneid* are excellent. But as for the pious Aeneas, the strong Cloanthes, the trusty Achates, the little Ascanius, the idiotic King Latinus, the bourgeois Amata, the insipid Lavinia, I can imagine nothing more cold or unpleasant. I prefer Tasso and the fantasy stories of Ariosto."

"Dare I ask, Sir," said Candide, "if you do not take pleasure in reading Horace?"

"Some of his maxims," said Pococurante, "can be of use to a man of the world, and since they are compressed into energetic verse, they easily become engraved in the memory. But I care very little about his journey to Brundisium, or his description of a bad dinner, or the quarrel between two ruffians, one named something like Pupilus, whose words, he says, *were full of pus,* and the other whose words *were like vinegar.* I can read only with extreme disgust his coarse verses against old women and witches, and I do not see what merit there can be in telling his friend Maecenas that if the latter places him in the ranks of lyric poets, he will strike the stars with his sublime forehead. Fools admire everything in an author who has a good reputation. I read only for myself; I like only what I can use."

Candide, who had been brought up never to judge anything for himself, was astonished by what he heard. Martin found Pococurante's way of thinking quite reasonable.

"Oh, here is Cicero," said Candide. "This great man—I can't imagine that you tire of reading him?"

"I never read him," replied the Venetian. "What does it matter to me if he defended Rabirius and Cluentius? I have enough lawsuits of my own to deal with. I was more inclined to appreciate his philosophical works, but when I saw that he doubted everything, I concluded that I already knew as much as he, and that I did not need anyone's help to become ignorant."

"Ah, here are eighty volumes of the proceedings of a scientific academy," exclaimed Martin. "There may be some good things in there."

"There would be," said Pococurante, "if any of the authors of this hotchpotch had invented even a new way of producing pins. But there is nothing in these books except vain theoretical systems, and not a single useful thing."

"Look at all those plays over there!" said Candide. "In Italian, Spanish, French!"

"Yes," said the Senator, "there are three thousand, and not three dozen good ones. As for those collections of sermons, which as a whole are not worth one page of Seneca, and all those thick volumes of theology, you may be sure that neither I, nor anybody else, ever opens them."

Martin noticed some shelves loaded with English books.

"I suppose," he said, "that a republican would derive pleasure from most of these books written in defense of freedom."

"Yes," said Pococurante, "it is noble to write what one thinks; it is the privilege of humankind. Throughout Italy people write only what they do not think. The inhabitants of the land of the Caesars and Antonines do not dare to have a single idea without the permission of a Dominican.[78] I would support the liberty that inspires English writers, if only selfishness and the spirit of faction did not corrupt all that is good in that precious freedom."[79]

Candide, noticing a volume of Milton, asked him if he did not regard this author as a great man.

"Who?" said Pococurante. "This barbarian who writes a long commentary on the first chapter of Genesis in ten books of harsh verse? This crude imitator of the Greeks who disfigures the Creation and who, even though the Scriptures represent the Eternal Being producing the universe with His words, has the Messiah pull out a big compass from a heavenly closet in order to design His work? Am I supposed to admire a man who spoils Tasso's images of Hell and the Devil? who disguises Lucifer sometimes as a toad, sometimes as a pygmy? who has him give the same speech a hundred times and makes him argue about theology? who takes so seriously Ariosto's comical story about the invention of firearms that he makes the demons shoot cannons in Heaven? Neither I nor anyone else in Italy could draw pleasure from such pitiful absurdities. The marriage of Sin and Death, and the snakes to which Sin gives birth, make any man vomit who has the slightest sense of good taste. And his long description of a hospital can be interesting only to gravediggers. This obscure, bizarre, and disgusting poem was despised when it was published; today I simply treat it as it was treated in the author's country by his contemporaries. Furthermore, I say what I think, and whether or not others agree matters very little to me."

[78]The Dominican friars organized the Inquisition.

[79]While advocating many forms of freedom, Voltaire was not in favor of popular participation in government. He believed that mass politics tended to degenerate into selfishness and factionalism.

Candide was distressed by these remarks. He respected Homer, and he liked Milton a bit.

"Alas!" he whispered to Martin, "I'm afraid this man may have an imperious contempt for our German poets."

"There's no harm in that," said Martin.

"Oh, what a superior man," Candide hissed. "What a great genius is this Pococurante! Nothing can please him."

After they had reviewed all the books in this manner, they went down into the garden. Candide praised the abundance of beauty.

"I know of nothing in such bad taste," said the Master. "We have nothing here but trifles; tomorrow I am going to redesign it on a nobler plan."

When the two curious travelers had taken leave of His Excellency, Candide said to Martin, "Well, you must admit that we just saw the happiest of men, for he is above everything he possesses."

"Don't you see," said Martin, "that he is disgusted with everything he possesses? Plato said a long time ago that the best stomachs are not those which refuse all food."

"But," said Candide, "isn't there joy in criticizing everything, in perceiving faults where other people think they see beauties?"

"That's to say," replied Martin, "that there is joy in having no joy?"

"Oh well!" said Candide. "So the only happy person in the world will be myself, when I see Miss Cunégonde again."

"It's always a good thing to hope," said Martin.

Yet the days flowed by, and then the weeks. Cacambo did not appear, and Candide was so immersed in his own sorrow that he did not even wonder why Paquette and Brother Giroflée had never returned to thank him.

CHAPTER 26

How Candide and Martin had supper with six foreigners, and who they were

One evening when Candide, accompanied by Martin, was about to sit down to eat with the foreigners who were lodging in the same hotel, a man whose face was the color of soot came up behind him, took him by the arm, and said, "Be ready to leave with us, do not fail."

Candide turned and saw Cacambo. Nothing but the sight of Cunégonde could have surprised and pleased him more. He nearly went mad with joy. He embraced his dear friend.

"Cunégonde must surely be here. Where is she? Take me to her, let me die of joy with her."

"Cunégonde isn't here," said Cacambo, "she's in Constantinople."

"Good heavens! In Constantinople! But even if she were in China, I'd leave in a second; let's go!"

"We'll leave after supper," replied Cacambo. "I can't tell you more. I'm a slave. My Master awaits me, I must wait on him. Don't say a word. Eat and be ready."

Candide, his heart pounding, his mind in turmoil, torn between joy and sorrow, delighted to see his faithful agent again and astonished to find him a slave, and filled with the thought of finding his mistress again, sat down with Martin, who was observing these events coolly, and with six foreigners who had come to spend the carnival season in Venice.

Cacambo, who was pouring the drinks for one of these foreigners, leaned toward his Master near the end of the meal and said, "Sire, Your Majesty may leave when he wishes; the ship is ready."

Having said these words, he walked away. The astonished guests looked at each other without uttering a single word. Then another servant approached his Master and said, "Sire, Your Majesty's carriage is in Padua and the boat is ready."

The Master gestured and the servant left. The other guests looked at each other again, and their mutual surprise redoubled. A third valet likewise approached a third foreigner and said, "Sire, I assure you, Your Majesty should not stay here any longer. I will prepare everything." And he promptly disappeared.

By now Candide and Martin were sure it was a carnival masquerade. A fourth servant said to the fourth Master, "Your Majesty may depart when he wishes," and left like the others. The fifth valet said the same thing to a fifth Master. But the sixth valet spoke differently to the sixth foreigner, who was seated next to Candide: "I swear, Sire, they will not give any more credit to Your Majesty, or to me; we could easily be locked up tonight, you and I. I am going to take care of my own affairs. Farewell."

With all the servants gone, the six foreigners, Candide, and Martin remained in deep silence. Finally Candide broke through it.

"Gentlemen," said he, "this is a remarkable jest. Why are you all behaving like royalty? I assure you that neither I nor Martin is a King."

It was Cacambo's master who spoke up gravely, saying in Italian, "I am not jesting. My name is Achmet III. I was the Grand Sultan for many years; I dethroned my brother; my nephew dethroned me; my viziers[80] had their throats cut; I am permitted to finish out my life in my old harem;

---

[80]Court officials.

my nephew, the current Grand Sultan, Mahmoud, allows me to travel; and I have come to spend the carnival season in Venice."[81]

The young man next to Achmet spoke next, "My name is Ivan; I was Emperor of all the Russias; I was dethroned as an infant; my mother and father were locked up; I was reared in jail; I sometimes get permission to travel, in the company of guards; and I have come to spend the carnival season in Venice."

The third said, "I am Charles Edward, King of England; my father ceded me his rights to the kingdom; I struggled to maintain them; the hearts of eight hundred of my supporters were ripped out and thrown in their faces; I was put in prison; I am going to Rome to visit the King, my father, who was dethroned like me and my grandfather; and I have come to spend the carnival season in Venice."

The fourth then spoke up: "I am the King of the Poles; the fortunes of war deprived me of my hereditary states; my father experienced the same reversal; I resign myself to Providence like Sultan Achmet, Emperor Ivan, and King Charles Edward, may they be granted long lives; and I have come to spend the carnival season in Venice."

The fifth said: "I am also King of the Poles; I lost my kingdom twice; but Providence has given me another state, where I have done more good than all of the Kings of the Sarmatians were able to do on the banks of the Vistula; I too resign myself to Providence; and I have come to spend the carnival season in Venice."

It remained for the sixth monarch to speak.

"Gentlemen," said he, "I am not as a great a Master as you are, but even so, I too was once a King. I am Theodore; I was elected King of Corsica; I used to be called 'Your Majesty,' and now I am lucky if I am called 'Sir'; I used to mint new coins, and now I am penniless; I used to have two secretaries of state and now I do not even have a valet; I used to sit on a throne and I ended up lying for years on straw in a London prison. I fear I will be treated the same here, though I have come, like Your Majesties, to spend the carnival season in Venice."

The five other Kings listened to this speech with noble compassion. Each gave King Theodore twenty sequins[82] to obtain suits and shirts. Candide presented him with a diamond worth two thousand sequins.

"Who is this ordinary citizen," said the five Kings, "who is in a position to give a hundred times more than any of us, and who voluntarily gives it?"

---

[81]All the kings mentioned in this chapter were real eighteenth-century rulers who lost their thrones.

[82]A Venetian gold coin.

Just as they were leaving the table, there arrived at the same hotel four other Serene Highnesses who had also lost their states through the fortunes of war, and who had come to spend the rest of the carnival season in Venice. But Candide took no notice of these newcomers. His only concern was to go find his dear Cunégonde in Constantinople.

CHAPTER 27

Candide's voyage to Constantinople

Faithful Cacambo had convinced the Turkish captain who was taking Sultan Achmet to Constantinople to admit Candide and Martin on board. The two of them embarked after prostrating themselves before His Miserable Highness. On the way, Candide said to Martin:

"We had supper with six dethroned Kings, and I even gave alms to one of them. Perhaps there are many other Princes even more unfortunate. As for me, I've only lost a hundred sheep, and I am flying into the arms of Cunégonde. My dear Martin, once again Pangloss was right: all is well."

"I wish it were so," said Martin.

"But," said Candide, "that was an extraordinary adventure we just had in Venice. No one before ever saw six dethroned Kings dining together in an inn or even heard of such a thing."

"It is no more extraordinary," said Martin, "than most of the things that have happened to us. It is very common for Kings to be dethroned. And as for the honor we had to dine with them, that is a trifle unworthy of our attention. What does it matter with whom you have supper, as long as you eat well?"[83]

Scarcely was Candide on the ship than he embraced his old valet, his friend Cacambo.

"Well, what is Cunégonde doing?" he asked him. "Is she still a marvel of beauty? Does she still love me? Is she in good health? Surely you have bought a palace in Constantinople for her?"

"My dear master," answered Cacambo, "Cunégonde is scrubbing dishes on the shores of the Propontis[84] for a Prince who has very few dishes. She's a slave in the household of a former Sovereign named Ragotski. He is in exile and the Grand Turk supports him with three

[83]The last line of this paragraph did not appear in any edition of the text published in Voltaire's lifetime. It comes from the so-called Wagnière manuscript—corrections found among Voltaire's papers after he died.
[84]An old name for the Sea of Marmara.

crowns a day. But what is even worse, she has lost her beauty and become horribly ugly."

"Ah! beautiful or ugly," said Candide, "I am an honorable man, and I am bound to love her forever. But how was she reduced to such an abject condition when I gave you five or six million?"

"All right," said Cacambo, "I had to give two million to Señor Don Fernando d'Ibaraa y Figueora y Mascarenes y Lampourdos y Souza, Governor of Buenos Aires, for permission to take back Miss Cunégonde. Then a pirate gallantly stole the rest. This pirate brought us to Cape Matapan, Melos, Nicaria, Samos, Petra, to the Dardanelles, Marmora, and Scutari. Cunégonde and the old woman are servants with that Prince I was telling you about, and I am a slave of the dethroned Sultan."

"What a horrifying series of calamities!" said Candide. "Yet, after all, I still have some diamonds. I will easily rescue Miss Cunégonde. What a pity that she's become so ugly."

Then turning toward Martin, he asked: "Which of us do you think is the most to be pitied, Emperor Achmet, Emperor Ivan, King Charles Edward, or me?"

"I have no idea," said Martin. "I would have to be inside your hearts to know."

"Ah!" said Candide. "If Pangloss were here, he would know, and he would tell us what to think."

"I don't know," said Martin, "what kind of scales your Pangloss had for weighing the miseries of humankind, and for appraising their pains. The one thing I take for granted is that there are millions of people on earth who are a hundred times more to be pitied than King Charles Edward, Emperor Ivan, and Sultan Achmet."

"That may well be true," said Candide.

In a few days they arrived in the Bosporus. Candide began by purchasing Cacambo's liberation at a high price. Then, without wasting any time, he flung himself and his companions into a galley ship[85] to go search for Cunégonde on the shores of Propontis, however ugly she might be.

Among the crew condemned to the galleys were two convicts who were rowing very badly, and upon whose bare shoulders the Levantine Captain occasionally applied a few lashes of a bullwhip. Naturally intrigued, Candide looked at them more closely than the other convicts and moved toward them with pity. Some features of their disfigured faces

---

[85]Galley ships were large military or transport vessels powered by slaves, prisoners of war, and convicted criminals who rowed under the harshest conditions. The ship in this chapter is a Turkish galley, but France too had galley ships, though they were few in number by the mid-eighteenth century.

struck him as having a slight resemblance to Pangloss and that unfortunate Jesuit, that Baron, that brother of Miss Cunégonde. This image moved and saddened him. He looked at them again more closely.

"Truly," he said to Cacambo, "if I hadn't seen the hanging of Dr. Pangloss, and if I hadn't had the misfortune of killing the Baron, I would swear that they are rowing in this galley."

At the words "Baron" and "Pangloss," the two convicts let out a loud cry, stopped rowing, and dropped their oars. The Levantine Captain rushed over with the whip and redoubled his strokes.

"Stop, stop, Sir," cried Candide. "I will give you as much money as you want."

"What! It's Candide!" cried one of the convicts.

"What! It's Candide!" cried the other.

"Is this a dream?" said Candide. "Am I awake? Am I really on this ship? Is that the Baron whom I killed? Is that Dr. Pangloss whom I saw hanged?"

"It is, it is!" they replied.

"What! Is that the great philosopher?" said Martin.

"Now, Mr. Levantine Captain," said Candide, "how much money do you want for the ransom of the gentleman from Thunder-ten-tronckh, one of the leading Barons of the Empire, and Mr. Pangloss, the most profound metaphysician of Germany?"

"Dog of a Christian," answered the Levantine captain, "since these two dogs of Christian slaves are Barons and metaphysicians, which is obviously a great honor in your country, you will give me fifty thousand sequins for them."

"You shall have them, Sir. Take me in a flash back to Constantinople, and you will be paid on the spot. No, take me first to Lady Cunégonde."

But after Candide's first offer, the Levantine Captain had already turned the prow toward the city, and the oars began to move faster than a bird's wings cleave the air.

Candide embraced the Baron and Pangloss a hundred times. "How is it that I didn't kill you, my dear Baron? And my dear Pangloss, how is it that you're alive after being hanged? And why are you both on the Turkish galleys?"

"Is it really true that my dear sister is in this country?" asked the Baron.

"Yes," replied Cacambo.

"At last I have found my dear Candide," cried Pangloss.

Candide introduced them to Martin and Cacambo. Everyone embraced, everyone spoke at the same time. The galley ship flew swiftly, and soon they were in the port. They summoned a Jew, who paid fifty thousand sequins for one of Candide's rings worth a hundred thousand, and who swore by Abraham that he could not offer more. Candide immediately paid the ransom for the Baron and Pangloss. The latter threw himself at his liberator's feet and bathed them with tears; the former thanked him with a nod and promised to pay back the money at the first opportunity.

"But is it really possible that my sister is in Turkey!" he asked.

"Nothing is more possible," Cacambo answered, "because she is scrubbing dishes for a Transylvanian prince."

They promptly summoned two Jews. Candide sold two more diamonds, and they all set out in another galley ship to rescue Miss Cunégonde.

CHAPTER 28

What happened to Candide, Cunégonde, Pangloss, Martin, etc.

"Forgive me once again," said Candide to the Baron. "Forgive me, my Reverend Father, for having run you through with a thrust of my sword."

"Forget about it," said the Baron. "I was a bit too hasty, I admit. But since you want to know how fortune brought me to the galleys, I will tell you. After my wound was cured by an apothecary, who was a brother in the Jesuit college, I was captured in a Spanish raid, abducted, and imprisoned in Buenos Aires just at the time my sister left. I asked permission to return to Rome to work in the Father General's office. Instead, I was sent to Constantinople to be the chaplain in the French ambassador's office. One evening, scarcely a week after I took up my new position, I met a young, good-looking page in the Sultan's court. It was hot. The young man wished to have a bath, and I took the opportunity to have one too. I did not know that it was a capital crime for a Christian to be found naked with a young Muslim. A cadi[86] sentenced me to be beaten a hundred times with a cane on the soles of the feet, and condemned me to the galleys. I do not think there has ever been a more horrible miscarriage of justice. But I would like to know why my sister is in the kitchen of a Transylvanian Sovereign who is in exile among the Turks."

"And you, my dear Pangloss," said Candide, "how is it that I am able to see you again?"

"It is true," said Pangloss, "that you saw me hanged. Of course, I was supposed to be burned, but you will recall that it began to rain heavily

---

[86]A Muslim judge.

when they were preparing to cook me. The storm was so violent that they lost hope of kindling the fire. They hanged me because they could do no better. A surgeon purchased my corpse, brought me home, dissected me. First he made a cross-shaped incision from my navel up and out to my collarbones. Never had a man been hanged more poorly than I had been. The Executioner for High Affairs of the Holy Inquisition, a subdeacon, really knew how to burn people with style, but he was not accustomed to hanging them. The rope was wet and did not slip smoothly; it became knotted; in short, I was still breathing. The cross-shaped incision released such a great cry from inside me that my surgeon fell over backward. Thinking that he was dissecting the Devil, he ran out, in mortal terror, falling down the staircase as he left. His wife rushed in from a nearby room when she heard the commotion. She saw me lying on the table with my cross-shaped incision. Even more frightened than her husband, she fled and stumbled over him as she left. When they had calmed down a bit, I heard her say to him, 'My dear, whatever led you to dissect a heretic? Don't you know, the Devil is always in the bodies of those people? I am going to get a priest to exorcise him right away.'

"I shuddered at these words, and I gathered whatever strength I still had left to call out, 'Take pity on me!' Finally the Portuguese barber took courage. He sewed up my skin. His wife even took care of me. I was on my feet in two weeks. The barber found me a job as lackey to a Knight of Malta who was headed for Venice. But my Master had no money to pay me, so I began to work for a Venetian merchant, and I accompanied him to Constantinople.

"One day I had an impulse to go into a mosque. It was empty except for an old imam and a very pretty young worshipper saying her prayers. Her bosom was completely uncovered, and between her breasts was a lovely bouquet of tulips, roses, anemones, buttercups, hyacinths, and primroses. She dropped her bouquet. I picked it up and I put it back in place with meticulous care. I took so much time replacing it that the imam became angry, and when he saw that I was a Christian he called for help. They brought me before the cadi, who sentenced me to a hundred strokes with a cane on the soles of the feet, and condemned me to the galleys. I was chained up in the very same galley ship and behind the same oar as the Baron. In that galley there were also four young men from Marseilles, five Neapolitan priests, and two monks from Corfu, who told us that similar things occurred every day. The Baron claims that he has endured greater injustice than I. I argue, however, that it is more lawful to replace a bouquet of flowers on a young woman's bosom than to be naked with a young male page. We were debating the question constantly and receiving twenty lashes of the bullwhip per day, when the chain of events of this universe led you to our galley in order to ransom us."

"Well, my dear Pangloss," Candide said, "when you were being hanged, dissected, beaten black and blue, and when you were rowing in the galleys, did you still think that everything is for the best in this world?"

"I still hold to my original opinion," replied Pangloss. "For after all, I am a philosopher, and it is not appropriate for me to take back my word. Leibniz is never mistaken. Moreover, preestablished harmony is the finest aspect of the universe, along with the plenum and subtle matter."[87]

CHAPTER 29

How Candide found Cunégonde and the old woman again

While Candide, the Baron, Pangloss, Martin, and Cacambo were reciting their adventures, theorizing about contingent and noncontingent events in the universe, and having debates about cause and effect, moral and physical evil, free will and determinism, and the consolations available to a galley slave in Turkey, they landed on the shore of the Propontis and came to the house of the Transylvanian Prince. The first thing they saw was Cunégonde and the old woman hanging towels on a line to dry.

The Baron turned pale at this sight. Candide, the tender lover, seeing his beautiful Cunégonde's swarthy complexion, bloodshot eyes, withered bosom, wrinkled cheeks, and peeling red skin, recoiled three paces in horror, then approached her out of respect for decency. She embraced Candide and her brother. They embraced the old woman, and Candide paid the ransom for her and Cunégonde.

There was a little farm in the area. The old woman suggested to Candide that they settle into it until the destiny of the group improved. Cunégonde did not know she had become ugly; no one told her. She reminded Candide of his promise in so firm a tone that the good Candide dared not refuse her. He thus informed the Baron of their intention to marry.

"I will never accept," said the Baron, "such baseness from her, and such insolence from you. I will not allow myself to be disgraced in this way. It would prevent my sister's children from entering the noble orders in Germany. No, never will my sister marry anyone but a Baron of the Empire."

---

[87]Preestablished harmony is one of Leibniz's concepts. The plenum and subtle matter were outdated notions in Cartesian physics that Newton had refuted.

Cunégonde threw herself at his feet and bathed them with tears. He was inflexible.

"You stubborn idiot," said Candide, "I rescued you from the galleys, I paid for your ransom and freed your sister. She was washing dishes here, and she's ugly. I have the generosity to make her my wife and you still protest against it. I would kill you again if I gave in to my anger."

"You may kill me again," said the Baron, "but you will never marry my sister while I am alive."

CHAPTER 30

Conclusion

In his heart, Candide had no desire to marry Cunégonde. But the Baron's extreme arrogance made him resolve to conclude the marriage, and Cunégonde pressed him so strongly that he could not take back his word. He consulted Pangloss, Martin, and the trusty Cacambo. Pangloss wrote a fine treatise in which he proved that the Baron had no legal rights over his sister and that, in accordance with all the laws of the Empire, she could marry Candide by the left hand.[88] Martin was in favor of throwing the Baron into the sea. Cacambo suggested they send him back to the Levantine Captain to serve his full term on the galleys, and then send him to the Father General in Rome on the first available ship. This idea was received very favorably. The old woman approved of it. They kept it secret from the Baron's sister. The plan was executed at a modest expense, and they had the pleasure of snaring a Jesuit and punishing the pride of a German baron at the same time.

It is quite natural to imagine that after so many disasters, Candide, now married to his mistress and living with the philosopher Pangloss, the philosopher Martin, the prudent Cacambo, and the old woman, and having also saved many diamonds from the land of the ancient Incas, must have enjoyed the most agreeable life in the world. But he was so cheated by the Jews that he soon found himself with nothing more than the little farm. His wife, growing uglier every day, became shrewish and intolerable. The old woman was infirm and even nastier than Cunégonde. Cacambo, who labored in the garden and traveled to Constantinople to sell vegetables, was worn out with toil and cursed his fate. Pangloss was

---

[88] A morganatic marriage between a noble and commoner in which the commoner and children acquire no noble rights.

in despair because he was not a star in some German university. As for Martin, fully persuaded that people are equally wretched everywhere, he bore life with patience.

Candide, Martin, and Pangloss sometimes debated metaphysical and moral issues. From the windows of the farm they often saw ships loaded with effendis, pashas, and cadis being exiled to Lemnos, Mytilene, and Erzerum. They saw other cadis, pashas, and effendis take the place of the exiles, and suffer exile in their turn. They saw heads being neatly impaled for presentation at the Sublime Port. These spectacles intensified their arguments, and when they were not debating, the boredom was so excessive that the old woman dared one day to say to them:

"I'd like to know which is worse—to be raped a hundred times by Negro pirates, to have a buttock cut off, to run the gauntlet among the Bulgars, to be whipped and hanged in an auto-da-fé, to be dissected, to row on the galleys, in short, to experience every misfortune we have known—or to stay here without anything to do?"

"That's a deep question," said Candide.

These remarks gave birth to new reflections, and it was Martin who concluded that human beings are destined to live in either convulsive anxiety or lethargic boredom. Candide did not accept this, but he offered no alternative. Pangloss admitted that he had always suffered horribly, but having once affirmed that everything in the world functioned marvellously, he kept affirming it, and never believed it.

One event especially served to confirm Martin in his dreadful principles, to make Candide hesitate more than ever before, and to embarrass Pangloss. It was the arrival at their farm of Paquette and Brother Giroflée, in the most extreme misery. They had quickly wasted their three thousand piastres; they had parted; come back together; quarreled; been put in prison; escaped; and in the end Brother Giroflée had become a Turk. Paquette practiced her trade throughout, and never earned anything.

"I was right," said Martin to Candide, "that your gifts would soon be squandered and would only make them more miserable. You were rolling in millions of piastres, you and Cacambo, and you were no happier than Brother Giroflée and Paquette."

"Ah! Ah!" said Pangloss to Paquette. "Heaven has brought you back to us, my poor child! Do you realize that you cost me the tip of my nose, an eye, and an ear? Look at you! Oh! What a world!"

This new adventure led them to philosophize more than ever.

There lived in the region a very famous dervish who was reputed to be the best philosopher in Turkey. They went to consult him. Pangloss spoke for everyone: "Master, we have come to ask you to tell us why such a strange animal as man was ever created."

"Why meddle in that?" said the dervish. "Is it any business of yours?"

"But Reverend Father," said Candide, "there is a horrible amount of evil in the world."

"What difference does it make," said the dervish, "if there is good or evil? When His Highness sends a ship to Egypt, does he worry about whether or not the mice are comfortable on board?"

"Then what is to be done?" said Pangloss.

"Keep silent," said the dervish.

"It was my humble expectation," said Pangloss, "that I could theorize a bit with you about effects and causes, the best of possible worlds, the origin of evil, the nature of the soul, and preestablished harmony."

At these words the dervish slammed the door in their faces.

During this conversation, news was spreading that the mufti and two viziers of the divan[89] had been strangled in Constantinople, and that many of their friends had been impaled. This catastrophe created a great uproar everywhere, for a few hours. Pangloss, Candide, and Martin, on their way back to the little farm, met a kindly old man, enjoying the fresh air by his door under a grove of orange trees. Pangloss, who was as curious as he was philosophical, asked him the name of the mufti who had just been strangled.

"I have no idea," replied the kindly old man, "and I have never known the name of any mufti or any vizier. I am entirely ignorant of the matter you refer to. I assume that in general those who meddle in public affairs perish, sometimes miserably, and that they deserve it. But I never think about what people are doing in Constantinople. I am content to sell them the fruits of the garden that I cultivate."

Having said these words, he invited the foreigners into his home. His two daughters and two sons served them several kinds of sherbet which they had made themselves, Turkish cream flavored with candied citron, oranges, lemons, limes, pineapples, pistachios, and mocha coffee unadulterated by the bad coffee of Batavia and the West Indies. Afterwards the kindly old Muslim's daughters sprinkled perfume on the beards of Candide, Pangloss, and Martin.

"You must possess," said Candide to the Turk, "a vast and magnificent estate?"

"I only have twenty acres," replied the Turk. I cultivate them with my

---

[89]The mufti is an expert on Muslim law; the viziers are court officials; the divan is a council of state.

children. Work keeps away three great evils: boredom, vice, and indigence."

While returning to his farm, Candide reflected deeply on the Turk's words. He said to Pangloss and Martin, "That kindly old man seems to have made a better life than the six kings we had the honor of eating supper with."

"Power and glory," said Pangloss, "are very dangerous, as all the philosophers tell us. For indeed, Eglon,[90] King of the Moabites, was assassinated by Ehud; Absalom was hanged by his hair and pierced with three spears; King Nadab, son of Jeroboam, was killed by Baasha; King Elah by Zimri; Ahaziah by Jehu; Athaliah by Jehoiada; Kings Jehoiakim, Jeconiah, and Zedekiah became slaves. You know how Croesus perished, and Astyages, Darius, Dionysius of Syracuse, Pyrrhus, Perseus, Hannibal, Jugurtha, Ariovistus, Caesar, Pompey, Nero, Otho, Vitellius, Domitian, Richard II of England, Edward II, Henry IV, Richard III, Mary Stuart, Charles I, the three Henrys of France, the Emperor Henry IV. You know ..."

"I know," said Candide, "that we must cultivate our garden."

"You are right," said Pangloss, "for when man was placed in the Garden of Eden, he was placed there *ut operaretur eum,* in order to work on it, which proves that humankind was not made for rest."

"Let us work without theorizing," said Martin. "That is the only way to make life bearable."

The little society entered into this laudable plan. Each began to exercise his talents. The little bit of earth became productive. Cunégonde was undeniably very ugly, but she baked excellent pastries. Paquette embroidered. The old woman took care of the linen. No one failed to contribute, not even Brother Giroflée. He was a very good carpenter and even became a sociable fellow.

And sometimes Pangloss would say to Candide, "All events are linked together in the best of all possible worlds. For after all, if you had not been driven from a fine castle with great kicks in the behind for loving Miss Cunégonde, if you had not been seized by the Inquisition, if you had not crossed South America on foot, if you had not thrust a sword into the Baron, if you had not lost your sheep from the good country of Eldorado, you would not be here eating candied citrons and pistachios."

"That is well said," replied Candide, "but we must cultivate our garden."

---

[90]All the rulers in this interminable list died by horrible means.

PART THREE

Related Documents

The following brief texts illustrate some aspects of the composition and reception of *Candide*. This is by no means a detailed documentary history. The intent is to supplement *Candide* with a few texts that reveal the emotional and intellectual intensity that Voltaire brought to the creative process—and the hardly less passionate reaction of his opponents.

VOLTAIRE

Letter to Catherine-Olympe du Noyer
November 28, 1713

In this letter to Catherine-Olympe du Noyer, nicknamed Pimpette, the nineteen-year-old Voltaire plans their elopement. They met in Holland when Voltaire was working as a secretary in the French embassy. The two did run away together as planned, but the adventure ended when Voltaire's father forced him to resume his law studies in Paris. Voltaire continued to write to Pimpette and tried to bring her to France. But Pimpette was reluctant to

Correspondence and Related Documents, ed. Theodore Besterman, in *The Complete Works of Voltaire* (Geneva: Institut et Musée Voltaire, 1968), 85:11–12.

leave Holland. Voltaire's passion gradually faded, and Pimpette married a man named Borillet in or about 1716.

The ardor and idealism of the youthful Voltaire make one think of Candide's adventure with Cunégonde. More than forty-five years later, when he was composing Candide, *Voltaire was still reflecting on the forbidden passion of his youth. As a Protestant, Pimpette was off limits for the Catholic Voltaire, just as Cunégonde, a noble, was off limits to the commoner Candide.*

I am a prisoner here in the name of the king. But they only have the power to take my life away, not my love for you. Yes, my adorable mistress, I will see you tonight, even if it brings my head to the chopping block. In the name of God, do not speak to me in the fatal tone in which you write to me. Live on, and be cautious. Be on your guard with your mother as you would with your most cruel enemy. What am I saying? Be on your guard with everyone; trust no one. Be ready as soon as the moon appears. I will leave the embassy *incognito*. I will take a coach or a chaise. We will fly like the wind to Schevelin. I will bring paper and ink. We will write the necessary letters. But if you love me, take heart. Summon all your virtue and all your presence of mind. Be discreet with your mother. Try to bring your portrait, and remember that preparation of the greatest tortures will not stop me from serving you. No, nothing is capable of separating me from you. Our love is based on virtue, it will last as long as our life. Order your shoemaker to find a chaise. But no, I do not want you to trust him. Be ready at four. I will wait for you near your street. Farewell, I will take any risk for you. You deserve much more. Farewell, my dear heart.

VOLTAIRE

Letter to Frederick, Crown Prince of Prussia
October 15, 1737

Voltaire began corresponding with Frederick, the Crown Prince of Prussia (later known as Frederick the Great) in 1736. He was then forty-one and Frederick twenty-four. Their correspondence lasted until the year of Voltaire's death and comprised more than seven hundred letters. Frederick was an

---

amateur poet and philosopher. He admired the teachings of Leibniz as popularized by Christian Wolff, which is to say that he believed that the world was governed by laws of necessity. In this letter, Voltaire expresses three key elements of his own philosophy. The first is his belief in free will, in other words, his conviction that people's conduct stems from choices, instead of being determined by external constraints. The second is his skepticism, or his tendency to doubt all theories which claim to have exact knowledge of the soul and God. Influenced by John Locke, Voltaire thought one can only know things one is able to perceive through the senses. Since the soul and God are inaccessible to the senses, he considered it pointless to attempt to describe their precise natures.

The third element is Voltaire's belief in universal principles of justice. These principles are rooted in the nature of human beings as creatures designed to live in "society." Voltaire argues that while human customs differ greatly around the world, all communities have rules that make social life possible. Some of the arguments for this social morality are a bit awkward in the letter below. In fact, there seems to be a tension between, on the one hand, Voltaire's skepticism regarding metaphysics and, on the other hand, his unshakable belief in justice — as if "justice" is concrete and discernible by the senses in a way that the "soul" and "God" are not. Yet this tension, this desire to make society ethical, is largely what kept Voltaire intellectually active and creative for so many decades. It is worth noting that at the end of Candide, *when the characters settle into cultivating their garden, they are described as forming a little "society."*

In this translation of Voltaire's letter to Frederick, I have omitted some lines from the original (as shown by ellipses).

Your Highness,

I have received the last letter, dated September 27, with which your Royal Highness honored me . . .

Your Highness, you ordered me to give you an account of my metaphysical doubts. I am taking the liberty of sending you an extract from a chapter on freedom [of the will]. Your Royal Highness will at least find sincerity in it, even if he perceives ignorance. And would to heaven that all ignorant people were at least sincere!

Humanity, which is the principle of all my thoughts, has perhaps led me astray in this work. Perhaps my idea that there would be neither vice nor virtue, that neither punishment nor reward would serve any purpose, that society, especially among philosophers, would be an exchange of wickedness and hypocrisy, if man did not have complete and absolute freedom [of the will] — I say, perhaps this opinion has carried me too far.

But if you find errors in my thoughts, forgive them for the sake of the principle that has produced them.

I always reduce, as much as I can, my metaphysics to ethics. I have sincerely examined, with all the care I am capable of, whether I can form any conceptions of the human soul; and I have seen that the fruit of all my research is ignorance. I find that my ideas about this thinking, free, and active being are about the same as my ideas about God himself. My reason tells me that God exists, but this same reason tells me that I cannot know what he is. Indeed, how could we know what our soul is, we who cannot even form any idea of light when we have the misfortune to be born blind? I observe, with sorrow, that everything ever written about the soul, fails to teach us the slightest truth . . . .

It is man whom I study. Whatever the materials that compose his inner nature may be, we must seek to know if vice and virtue are real. This is the important point with regard to man. I do not say with regard to a particular society living under particular laws, but for the entire human species: for you, Your Highness, who will someday rule, for the woodcutter in your forests, for the Chinese doctor, and for the American savage. Locke, the wisest metaphysician I know, while justifiably combating innate ideas, seems to think that there are no universal principles of morality. I dare to combat, or rather to clarify, the idea of this great man on this point. I agree with him that there are really no innate ideas. It follows logically that there are no innate moral propositions in our soul. But simply because we are not born with beards, does it follow that we, the inhabitants of this continent, were not born to be bearded at a certain age? We are not born with the strength to walk. But everyone born with two feet will walk one day. In the same way, no one carries with him at birth the idea that one must be just; but God has constructed the organs of men so that all of them, at a certain age, agree on this truth.

It is clear to me that God wanted us to live in society, just as he gave bees an instinct and instruments suited for making honey. Since our society cannot last without ideas of justice and injustice, he gave us the means to acquire them. Our different customs, it is true, will never allow us to attach the same idea of justice to identical conceptions. What is a crime in Europe will be a virtue in Asia, just as certain German stews give no pleasure to gourmets in France. But God has formed the Germans and French in such a way that they all like good cooking. All societies, then, will not have the same laws, but no society will be without laws. Thus the good of society is certainly established among all men, from Peking to Ireland, as the permanent standard of virtue: whatever is useful to society will therefore be good in each country. This single idea resolves at once all the apparent contradictions in human morality. Theft was permitted in Sparta, but why? Because property was held in common there, and to steal from a miser who kept for himself what the law assigned to the public was a service to society.

It is said that there are savages who eat men and think this is good conduct. My answer is that these savages have the same ideas we do of justice and injustice. They fight wars as we do out of rage and passion. One can see the same crimes committed everywhere: eating one's enemies is just an extra ceremony. The evil is not putting them on a spit; the evil is killing them. And I will venture to affirm that there is no savage who believes it is good behavior to cut his friend's throat. I once saw four savages from Louisiana who were brought to France in 1723. Among them was a woman with a very gentle disposition. I asked her through an interpreter if she had sometimes eaten the flesh of her enemies and if she had found it to her taste. She answered yes. I asked her if she would ever willingly kill, or order someone to kill, one of her compatriots in order to eat him. She began to tremble and responded with evident horror at the thought of such a crime. I defy those who have traveled around the world, even the most hardened liars, to dare to tell me that there is a single tribe or family where one is allowed to go back on one's word. I have good reason to believe that since God created some animals to graze in common, others to see each other rarely and only two at a time, and spiders to spin webs, every species has the instruments necessary for the work it must do. Just as man has been endowed with a stomach for digestion, eyes for sight, and a soul for judgment, so he is endowed with everything he needs to live in society . . .

I am with the deepest respect and most affectionate gratitude, etc.

VOLTAIRE

Letter to
François-Thomas-Marie de Baculard d'Arnaud
October 14, 1749

While most of Voltaire's philosophical ideas were fixed in the 1730s and 1740s, a new element of pessimism began to color his thought in the 1750s. As described in the introduction, the two events that did the most to intensify his tragic vision were the death of his mistress, Émilie du Châtelet, and the Lisbon earthquake. Voltaire communicated openly to his friends about these misfortunes. Arnaud, the recipient of the following letter, was a young writer and one of Voltaire's closest correspondents. Voltaire declares that his mistress was a "great man," thus indicating that he not only loved her as a woman but took her seriously as a thinker.

My dear child, a woman who translated and explained Newton and who had translated Virgil, yet without ever alluding in conversation to these achievements, a woman who never spoke ill of anyone and never uttered a lie, a friend whose friendship was constant and courageous—in a word, a very great man whom ordinary women only knew through her diamonds and dancing: for her you will never prevent my weeping all my life. I am very far from departing for Prussia; I can hardly leave the house. I am very touched by your sympathy. You have the kind of heart I need, so you may be certain that I care for you deeply. I ask you to transmit my respects to Monsieur de Morand. Farewell my dear d'Arnaud; I embrace you.

Correspondence and Related Documents, 95:178–79.

VOLTAIRE

Letter to Jean-Robert Tronchin
November 24, 1755

The recipient of the following letter about the Lisbon earthquake was a French banker and one of Voltaire's closest confidants.

This, sir, is a very cruel sort of physics. People will find it awkward indeed to explain how the laws of motion bring about such frightful disasters in "the best of possible worlds." A hundred thousand ants, our neighbors, crushed in a second in our ant-hill, and half of them undoubtedly perishing in inexpressible anguish in debris from which it was impossible to extricate them: families all over Europe ruined, the fortunes of a hundred merchants from your homeland swallowed up in the ruins of Lisbon. What a sad game of chance is the game of human life! What will the preachers say, especially if the palace of the Inquisition is still standing? I hope that at least the Reverend Fathers, the Inquisitors, have been crushed like the others. That ought to teach men not to persecute men, for while a few holy scoundrels burn a few fanatics, the earth swallows up them all.

I have already seen our friend Gauffecourt. I am going to Monrion as late as possible. I think our mountains are saving us from the earthquakes. Goodbye, my dear correspondent. Inform me, please, of the results of this horrible event.

Correspondence and Related Documents, 100:401–02.

OMER JOLY DE FLEURY

Letter to Henry-Léonard-Jean-Baptiste Bertin

February 24, 1759

The author of the following letter was a leading member of the Parlement of Paris, one of the institutions in France that possessed broad powers of censorship. The recipient was the head of the Paris police.

During the past several days, a brochure entitled *Candide, or Optimism, Translated from the German by Dr. Ralph,* has been circulating publicly. This brochure, of which I have been able to skim only a few chapters so far, seems to contain references and allusions contrary to religion and good morals. Moreover, I know that in good society, people are disgusted by the impieties and indecencies it contains. It is very surprising that some persist in trying to flood the public with such pernicious works, especially after the formal decree that the Parlement recently issued on works of this kind. Thus, I believe you ought to take the most prompt and severe measures to stop the sale of such a scandalous brochure and to uncover the authors. I implore you not to waste time, and to inform me if you find witnesses able to give testimony regarding the authors and distributors, so that I can have them questioned.

Correspondence and Related Documents, 103:426.

VOLTAIRE

Letter to Gabriel and Philibert Cramer

February 25, 1759

Voltaire wrote the following letter to the Cramers, his publishers, to protect himself from prosecution. The idea was that if he were put on trial, his publishers would produce this letter to prove that Voltaire was not the author of Candide! *Voltaire enjoyed this masquerade in which he pretended to be a naive observer of the scandals he created.*

Correspondence and Related Documents, 103:427.

What is this brochure entitled *Candide* which I hear is being sold with such scandal and which I hear comes from Lyons? I would very much like to see it. Gentlemen, could you get me a bound copy? Rumor says that there are people impertinent enough to attribute to me this work which I have never seen! I request that you tell me what the truth is.

ELIE FRÉRON

Review of Candide
1759

One of Voltaire's critics was Elie Fréron, the editor of the Année littéraire, *or* Literary Year. *In this clever review, Fréron plays along with Voltaire's denials that he wrote* Candide. *He pretends to prove that Voltaire could not be the author because* Candide *contains pessimistic ideas that contradict the optimism of Voltaire's other writings.* Candide *does contradict a few of Voltaire's own writings (see the introduction for fuller discussion), so Fréron succeeded in making Voltaire look inconsistent. But Voltaire did not claim that his ideas had always been the same.* Candide *is about a young man who undergoes change. Voltaire recognized change in himself and used the novel to express it. Fréron, then, missed the point entirely.*

Still, the review is worth reading. First, it contains lucid definitions of "optimism" and "pessimism." Second, it shows the popularity of forensic literature in the period—the public's hunger for scandalous propaganda written as if someone were being put on trial. (Fréron writes as if he were prosecuting the author of Candide *with Voltaire himself as principal witness.) Finally, the review conveys the aggressive and insulting tone of journalism in Voltaire's age. Voltaire was sensitive to such attacks and responded in kind. In 1761, he added a section to Chapter 22 of* Candide *in which Fréron appears as a "fat pig" who understands nothing about literature.*

Candide, or Optimism

No, Sir, I cannot believe that *Candide, or Optimism,* supposedly "translated from the German of Doctor Ralph," has been correctly attributed to the famous poet [Voltaire], no matter how clever you find it to be here and there. There is surely among us a malicious spirit who has studied the art of counterfeiting this illustrious author, and who beneath his mask is laughing at our error and the harm he is bringing to his model. Monsieur de Voltaire's frequent denials [that he wrote *Candide*] leave no doubt about the existence of this clever monkey. In painting, nothing is more common than attempts to copy this or that painter, efforts which greatly confuse our experts and often elicit risky and false judgments. Is it really the style of writing rather than the way of thinking, the arrangement of phrases rather than the consistency of principles, which most reveal the identity of a writer? As for myself, I am convinced that any work that contradicts all the maxims of an author cannot be by him. *Candide* is precisely a case in point in relation to the happy hermit of *Les Délices*.[1] The proof is irrefutable. Monsieur de Voltaire himself provides it. I believe that after his own testimony you will have nothing to say. All of his works are in my presence; I have just reread the whole numerous collection for reasons that will soon become clear to you. I will faithfully transcribe his words.

The word *Optimism,* from the Latin adjective *optimus* meaning the best, is applied to the doctrine of the philosophers, called *Optimists*, who agree with Leibniz and Father Malebranche that God made things in accordance with the perfection of his ideas, in other words, the best he could, and that if he could have improved upon his creation he would have done so. This opinion is inverted in *Candide.* Installed in its place is an absolutely opposed system, and the horrible conclusion to be drawn from the work is that this world is the worst of possible worlds. In short, instead of *Optimism,* it is *Pessimism,* if I may say so. But Monsieur de Voltaire is very far from admitting such an obvious absurdity! Listen to his doctrine.

[Several quotations from Voltaire's earlier writings follow, of which only three are translated here.]

"It is proven that there is more good than evil in this world because in fact few men desire death. You are thus wrong to complain on behalf of the human species and even more wrong to renounce your Sovereign under the pretext that some of his subjects are unhappy." ("On God," in *Mélanges de littérature.*)

"Man is not a riddle as some people claim, just so they can derive pleasure from trying to solve it. Man appears to have a place in nature . . . . He is, like everything we see, a mixture of evil and good, pleasure and pain. He has been given the passions in order to act, and reason in order to govern his actions. If man were perfect, he would be God. And those sup-

---

[1]This was the name of Voltaire's estate.

posed contrasts that you call contradictions are the necessary ingredients that enter into the composition of man, who is, like the rest of nature, what he must be." *(Remarques sur les Pensées de Pascal)*

"Our existence is not as miserable as some would like us to believe. To regard the universe as a dungeon is the idea of a fanatic . . . . To think that the earth, men, and the animals are what they must be in the order of Providence is, I believe, the mark of a wise man." (Ibid.)

Now Sir, I believe you must be convinced that *Candide,* in its philosophical aspect, cannot be by Monsieur de Voltaire.

The literary aspect furnishes another proof that this brochure did not issue from his pen. In his *Essay on Epic Poetry* he exalts the genius of Homer, Virgil, and Milton; he pronounces their names only with the admiration they deserve. The author of *Candide* places these great men in the ranks of the least important writers. [Here Fréron quotes Pococurante's words in Chapter 25 at length.] Horace and Cicero get treated just as badly. In good faith, Sir, is it imaginable that Monsieur de Voltaire, who has given us so much evidence of his respect for these gods of Parnassus, could speak of them with such irreverence?

Besides, the fabric of *Candide* is so unnatural that one must utterly reject the idea that he is the author. You know how little he thinks of those writers who abandon themselves to their insane imagination. "It is easier to portray ogres and giants than heroic men, and to distort nature instead of adhering to it." *(Essai sur la poësie epique)*

Finally, this novel is too rude in the moral aspect for anyone even to suspect that he composed it. Recall what he said about the indecency of Rabelais. "He is to be seen as first among the buffoons. It is irritating that a man with so much wit made such miserable use of it. He is a drunken philosopher who only wrote when he was drinking." *(Mélanges d'histoire et de philosophie)* "Woe unto him," he writes elsewhere, "who says everything he is capable of saying."[2]

Do you believe, Sir, that a man who has always defended the respect that he considers to be due to literature could, at the age of sixty-five, renounce this respect and imitate those youngsters who, as he says, begin "by producing great hopes and good works, and end by writing nothing but stupidities"? *(Mélanges de littérature)*

---

[2]No reference is given in the original for this quotation.

A Voltaire Chronology
(1694–1791)

1694   November 21: Voltaire born in Paris as François-Marie Arouet.

1704–11   Attends Jesuit college of Louis-le-Grand.

1710   Publication of Leibniz's *Theodicée* (Theodicy).

1715   Death of Louis XIV; France governed by a Regent, the duke of Orléans.

1716   Voltaire accused of a satire against the Regent.

1717   Imprisoned in the Bastille.

1718   First uses name "Voltaire." Stages his first play, *Oedipe* (Oedipus), and becomes a literary star.

1721   Montesquieu publishes *Les Lettres persanes* (The Persian Letters).

1723   Voltaire publishes *La Ligue* (The League), an epic poem about Henry IV, and is hailed now as a great poet as well as playwright.

1726   Voltaire quarrels with the Chevalier Rohan, is imprisoned in the Bastille, and then exiled to England.

1728   Returns to England.

1733   Pope's *Essay on Man.*

1734   Voltaire publishes *Lettres philosophiques* (Philosophical Letters); the work is condemned by the Parlement of Paris. Voltaire flees to Cirey and begins living with Madame du Châtelet.

1736   Begins correspondence with Frederick of Prussia.

1745   Becomes historiographer to Louis XV at Versailles.

1746   Elected to Académie Française.

1747   Publishes *Zadig,* his first *conte* or short novel (the genre to which *Candide* belongs); loses favor at court.

1748   Montesquieu publishes *De L'Esprit des lois* (The Spirit of the Laws).

1749   Death of Madame du Châtelet.

1750   Voltaire moves to Frederick the Great's court at Potsdam.

1751   First volume of the *Encyclopédie* (Encyclopedia, edited by Diderot and d'Alembert) appears in print.

1753   Voltaire leaves Frederick's court.

1755   Settles at Les Délices in Geneva. Lisbon earthquake.

1756   Publishes *Essai sur les moeurs* (Essay on Manners and Morals), a major historical work, and poem on the Lisbon earthquake.

1756–63   Seven Years' War.

1757   Damiens tries to assassinate Louis XV. John Byng shot in England.

1759   Publishes *Candide*; acquires chateau of Ferney near Geneva.

1762   Rousseau publishes *Du Contrat social* (The Social Contract) and *Émile*.

1764   Voltaire publishes *Dictionnaire philosophique* (Philosophical Dictionary).

1774   Death of Louis XV; succeeded by Louis XVI.

1778   Voltaire returns to Paris, dies May 30, buried secretly in Champagne.

1789   Beginning of the French Revolution.

1791   Voltaire's body transferred to the Pantheon in Paris.

Questions for Consideration

1. If you have read this book for a course and the readings included a textbook, how does the textbook define the Enlightenment? How does it portray Voltaire? Has reading *Candide* changed your conception of the Enlightenment and Voltaire? If so, explain how and why.

2. Consider Chapters 17 and 18 on Eldorado. How do these chapters represent Voltaire's vision of a good society? How does Eldorado differ from the European societies of the eighteenth century? Be sure to describe the moral and religious beliefs of the people in Eldorado. How do these resemble or contradict Christianity? If Eldorado is such a great place, why does Candide decide to leave it?

3. Explain the meaning of Martin's statement in Chapter 30, "Let us work without theorizing."

4. Discuss the techniques Voltaire uses to entertain his readers while he simultaneously forces them to confront difficult philosophical issues.

5. If you were a European monarch in the eighteenth century, which parts of *Candide* would you find most disturbing? What if you were a Jesuit? The pope? A Protestant? An aristocrat? An army general?

6. The references to Jews in *Candide* are consistently derogatory. (See, for example, the beginning of Chapter 9 and the last few paragraphs of Chapter 27.) On this basis, is it reasonable to say that Voltaire was anti-Semitic?

7. Read the letters by Voltaire translated in this volume. How do his letters differ from the usual type of letters people write today? Select one letter and discuss its purpose, its style, and its connections with *Candide*.

8. Read Fréron's review of *Candide* (translated in this volume) and discuss its strengths and weaknesses as a critique of the book.

9. Consider the great figures of eighteenth-century U.S. history: Franklin, Jefferson, and so on. Are any of them like Voltaire? Did any of them write stories like *Candide?* If not, how would you account for the fact that the United States did not produce a Voltaire? Is it because Voltaire was unique or because such a person could materialize only in an absolute monarchy like France?

Selected Bibliography

More has been written about Voltaire than about the history of most countries of the world. The works listed here are all readable, scholarly, and insightful. For a more systematic bibliography, a good starting place is *Pour encourager les autres: Studies for the Tercentenary of Voltaire's Birth, 1694–1994,* ed. Haydn Mason, vol. 320 of *Studies on Voltaire and the Eighteenth Century* (Oxford: Voltaire Foundation, 1994), pp. 163–318.

Gay, Peter. *Voltaire's Politics: The Poet as Realist* (New Haven: Yale University Press, 1988; first published in 1959 by Princeton University Press).

Goulemot, Jean, et al. (editors), *Inventaire Voltaire* (Paris: Gallimard, 1955). This book is in French.

Lanson, Gustave. *Voltaire* (Paris: Hachette, 1906); translated into English by Robert A. Wagoner (New York: John Wiley and Sons, 1966).

Mason, Haydn. *Voltaire: A Biography* (Baltimore: The Johns Hopkins University Press, 1981).

Pomeau, René. *Voltaire* (Paris: Seuil, 1955). This book is in French.

Starobinski, Jean. "Voltaire's Double-Barreled Musket," in *Blessings in Disguise; Or, The Morality of Evil,* translated from the French *(Le Remède dans le mal)* by Arthur Goldhammer (Cambridge: Harvard University Press, 1993), pp. 84–117.

Waldinger, Renée (editor), *Approaches to Teaching Voltaire's* Candide (New York: The Modern Language Association of America, 1987).

Index of Key Concepts

This is not a conventional index of names, places, and events. It is a thematic index designed to help readers perceive some of the recurrent ideas, phrases, and images in *Candide* and in the related documents written by Voltaire. (The Introduction and documents written by people other than Voltaire are not indexed here.) Some of the entries include more than one term, such as "disease, doctors, health, illness, medicine." Such groupings are what lexicographers call "semantic fields" — clusters of terms that highlight an area of reality or that articulate an abstract ideal. It seems more convenient to list the entire semantic field at once instead of listing each term individually and creating complicated cross-references.

Africans, 61, 62, 64, 65, 70, 82, 83
all is well, best of all worlds,
    optimism, preestablished
    harmony, 42, 43, 47, 48, 49, 50,
    52, 53, 57, 59, 74, 78, 83, 85, 94,
    99, 110, 115, 118, 119, 127

beauty, 42, 56, 60, 61, 63, 66, 80, 95,
    103, 107, 110, 111, 115
books, reading, 93, 94, 104, 105, 106,
    107
boredom, 86, 117, 119

cannibalism, 64, 65, 74, 75, 125
cause and effect, 42, 43, 46, 48, 51,
    115
ceremony, etiquette, politeness,
    sociability, urbanity, 77, 80, 85,
    88, 93, 103, 119
charity, 46, 49, 54, 109
commerce, merchants, 63, 77, 83, 85,
    86, 88, 114

cooking, food, 43, 44, 48, 52, 53, 54,
    55, 57, 61, 69, 72, 73, 77, 80, 85,
    86, 90, 91, 94, 100, 101, 104, 107,
    108, 110, 118, 119

diamonds, gold, jewels, money,
    treasure, 44, 49, 50, 51, 58, 61, 62,
    67, 69, 76, 77, 78, 79, 80, 81, 82,
    84, 85, 86, 87, 88, 89, 90, 93, 95,
    96, 97, 109, 111, 112, 113, 114,
    116, 117
disease, doctors, health, illness,
    medicine, 45, 48, 49, 50, 70, 90,
    91, 96, 101, 110, 114
dump, 58, 91, 101

earthquakes, 51, 52, 56, 64
equality, 59, 71, 79
evil, 66, 86, 99, 115, 118, 125

free will, 45, 52, 89, 115, 123

137

garden, 116, 118, 119
god, religion, 79, 87, 88, 124, 125
government, laws, 79, 81, 91, 124

happiness, joy, pleasure, 42, 68, 70, 76, 78, 81, 82, 84, 87, 88, 91, 96, 100, 102, 104, 107, 108, 117
hope, 60, 86, 107
humanity, 123

injustice, 86, 114
Inquisition, inquisitors, 52, 53, 56, 57, 58, 59, 67, 71, 73, 84, 114, 119, 127
insanity, 98
international law, 46, 61, 75
Islam, 62, 65, 113, 114

Jesuits, 48, 59, 68, 69, 70, 71, 72, 73, 74, 75, 112, 113, 116
Jews, 53, 56, 57, 58, 65, 67, 71, 84, 112, 113, 116
justice, 50, 68, 75, 113, 124, 125

kings, royalty, 68, 76, 77, 80, 108, 109, 110, 119

Leibniz, 115
liberty, 45, 52, 81, 106
Locke, 124
love, passion, 44, 48, 57, 58, 59, 60, 61, 66, 73, 88, 89, 92, 95, 96, 100, 101, 110, 111, 119, 122

Manicheanism, 97
melancholy, misery, misfortune, pain, sorrow, suffering, unhappiness, 48, 50, 54, 55, 60, 61, 65, 67, 72, 81, 83, 84, 85, 86, 87, 92, 95, 96, 98, 100, 101, 102, 103, 107, 108, 111, 117
metaphysics, philosophers, philosophy, theory, 42, 45, 46, 49, 50, 51, 53, 57, 58, 59, 79, 88, 89, 91, 95, 104, 105, 112, 115, 116, 117, 118, 119, 123, 124
monks, 48, 59, 67, 68, 79, 100, 101, 102, 117
music, 63, 104

natural law, nature, state of nature, 41, 46, 48, 49, 74, 75, 78, 104, 124
nobility, lineage, 41, 60, 65, 66, 67, 71, 73, 89, 92, 93, 115

painting, 103, 104
plague, 64
popes, 47, 60, 64, 65, 91
priests, 42, 79, 90, 114
property, 50, 125

sciences, 43, 80, 81, 82, 105
slavery, 61, 64, 83, 108, 110, 111, 112, 115, 119
society, 119, 124, 125
soul, 41, 124
sufficient reason, 43, 45, 48, 49, 51
suicide, 65

theater, 91, 94, 106

virtue, 56, 82, 100, 122, 123, 124

war, 45, 46, 48, 49, 62, 64, 65, 68, 87, 95, 98, 99, 110
women, 47, 56, 62, 66, 68, 73, 79, 90, 126